For Diana — keep laughing!

# MEN FAKE FOREPLAY

### ...AND OTHER LIES THAT ARE TRUE

**━━ Written by ━━**

# MIKE DUGAN

**EMMY AWARD—WINNING WRITER AND COMEDIAN**

Best,

Mike Dugan

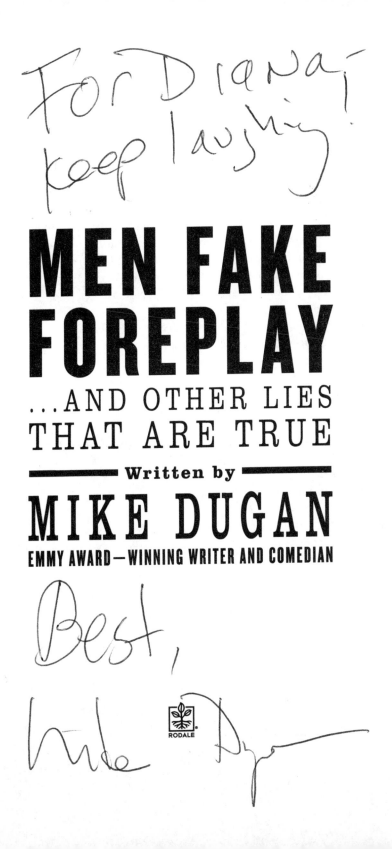

RODALE

# For Shari, Aidan, and Keiran

. . .

Book design by Susan P. Eugster

**Library of Congress Cataloging-in-Publication Data**

Dugan, Mike.
  Men fake foreplay : —and other lies that are true / Mike Dugan.
     p.     cm.
  ISBN 1–59486–074–2  hardcover
  1. Men—Humor.   2. Man-woman relationships—Humor.   I. Title.
PN6231.M45D84   2004
814′.6—dc22
                                                      2004016647

**Distributed to the trade by Holtzbrinck Publishers**

2   4   6   8   10   9   7   5   3   1   hardcover

 **RODALE**

WE INSPIRE AND ENABLE PEOPLE TO IMPROVE
THEIR LIVES AND THE WORLD AROUND THEM

FOR MORE OF OUR PRODUCTS
WWW.**RODALESTORE**.COM
(800) 848-4735

# CONTENTS

iii

A man's got to know his limitations.

—DIRTY HARRY

# WHERE'S THE HEAT?

If you always do
what you always did,
you will always get
what you always got.
**—GEORGE O'HAGAN**

**A**bout 10 years ago, I headed to a monastery in the hills above Santa Barbara to attend a weekend retreat led by a Native American spiritualist. I had just screwed up yet another relationship, and I needed all the help I could get. The spiritualist was also a retired NASA engineer, a background that gave him a uniquely scientific approach to examining and explaining spirituality.

Over the course of the weekend, he told us that heat-seeking missiles don't actually seek heat. Rather, a heat-seeking missile senses when it's heading away from the heat and adjusts itself, returning to the heat. It's designed to make mistakes and correct itself. It's called a teleological system.

Then he told us that human beings are teleological systems. It's our nature to make mistakes and correct them. It's the way we're built.

He said that unlike people, the missile doesn't beat up on itself when it makes a mistake. It accepts its nature. If people could understand that we are designed to make mistakes and learn from them, we would be much less judgmental of ourselves. It's a beautiful lesson in forgiveness and self-acceptance.

So, I wondered, what about the idiots who keep making the same mistakes over and over again? And why am I one of them?

Well, it turns out there are a few more things the missile won't do: The missile won't try to blame another missile for its problems. It won't lie and make up excuses. It won't tell you you're overreacting. It won't rationalize its behavior. It won't get sarcastic. It won't chuckle dismissively and tell you "You're imagining things" when you're not. And it certainly won't start seeking other, younger, prettier targets.

And just in case you're beginning to think this book is about bashing men, the missile also doesn't conclude that all targets are assholes who think with their dicks.

This book is about preconceptions that block us from intimacy. This book is about being open to change. This book is about heading back to the heat.

And who the hell is George O'Hagan?

**fore·play** (fōr-plā, fôr-) 1929 n.
1. sexual stimulation prior to intercourse.
2. action or behavior that precedes an event.

I looked up *foreplay* in Webster's dictionary. The first thing I noticed was that the word *foreplay* entered the dictionary in 1929. The year the stock market crashed. I'm not sure of the connection, but I have a feeling that when men lose their money, they begin to realize it might be a good idea to be more considerate to women.

The fact that *foreplay* entered the dictionary in 1929 tells me one of two things. Either there was no such thing as the act of foreplay before 1929, or they had foreplay but needed to come up with a word for it so women could finally ask for what they weren't getting. Not that it would help much, as it turns out. But knowing precisely what it is you're missing is better than a nagging and indefinable emptiness. I think.

Consider again, please, the year 1929. In 1929 the Model T Ford was state-of-the-art transportation. The new talking movies were all the rage. Music was played on Victrolas. Vibrators ran on kerosene.

Much has changed in the years since 1929. Civilization has made astronomical advances in technology. We have explored the vastness of space and discovered the building blocks of life. But our view of foreplay has remained as limited as life in 1929.

Let's go in and dust it off. Let's take a new look. Let's look past the sexual definition of foreplay that we all know and love and take a good look at that second definition: "Action or behavior that precedes an event."

Oh, and by the way,
women don't "take longer."
Women last longer.

# BEDFORD
# FALLS

**M**y mom and dad love each other. They've been married for 55 years. My father has always said that the key to a good marriage is communication. Over the course of their marriage, Mom and Dad have really honed their communication skills: They talk to each other through the dog now.

I noticed it the last time I went home to visit. My mom was three feet from my dad, and she looked down at the dog. "Your father needs to clean up the garage, doesn't he? *Yes. He. Does.*"

That dog used to be me. They used to talk to each other like that through their kids all the time. Although I imagine it has to be especially tough on the dog. A minute of that is like seven minutes to a dog.

Therapists call that style of communication "triangulation." It's against the rules of therapy, but what did my parents' generation know about relationship skills? They didn't have time for theory. They flew by the seat of their pants. They were among the millions of parents who were busy raising the baby boomers.

My parents came out of World War II and headed straight for the suburbs to raise a family. It was practically their patriotic duty. They reproduced for the flag, and the Catholic Church cheered them on. Millions of young newlyweds had the same idea: Use a loan from the GI Bill to buy a house near the train that will take you to work in the city so you can make the money to pay for the house that's near the train that will take you to work in the city so you can . . . provide a better life for your children than the one you had.

They both had grown up in poverty, and they were determined to sacrifice so their children could flourish. It was part stoic work ethic and part Catholic martyrdom. As my parents made clear to us several times a day, "Everything we do, we do for you kids."

Maude and Ray Dugan eventually had three girls and two boys. They did their best with us. They tried; they really did. But there were five of us and only two of them; they were outnumbered.

I was the youngest and the most trouble. If you're from a big family, you know that by the time parents get down to the youngest child, leniency has set in. They give up. They just say, "Hell with it. What's your name again? Go do some work."

My brother would get grounded for being 10 minutes late for dinner. By the time they got around to me, it was pretty much "No heroin in the living room."

"Michael? You're not using the *good* spoons, are you?"

I had a great deal of potential as a child. I know, because it said so on my report cards every six weeks. I can remember thinking that somewhere there had to be a parent who got their kid's report card home, opened it up, and read, "Your child has absolutely no potential whatsoever. We'd hold him back a year, but it's a waste of milk."

If you are a kid and you have potential, you are doing your job. I always wondered at what point in your life possession of potential is no longer enough to validate your existence: "He's got potential."

"Are you kidding? He's 80 years old and hasn't done a thing."

"Yeah, but I'm pulling for him. I think he's got it in him. You know, it's cynics like you who kill a man's spirit."

Are you beginning to wonder what all this has to do with foreplay? Jeez. Would you please just lie back and relax?

My parents' plan was to move to a nice neighborhood in a town with a good school system, and the schools and church would help raise the kids right. They believed in community, and they found their community in Ramsey, New Jersey.

Many people have a bad impression of New Jersey because they fly into Newark Airport and see the refineries and chemical plants and think that's what New Jersey is. Some of these people will even tell you it's called the Garden State because if you breathe the air and drink the water long enough, you will turn into a vegetable. But the actual reason New Jersey is called the Garden State is because if you wrong the wrong people, they will plant you in the Meadowlands.

Clearly, my parents weren't the only ones chasing the American dream to the suburbs. Living within the 30 houses on our cul-de-sac street were 72 children under the age of 18. There was always someone to play with and always much playing to be done.

Out on the street, a car would drive by maybe once every 15 minutes and we'd have to move the backstop used for our baseball game. If it was Mr. Eberling's car, we probably gave him a dirty look because he was the guy who yelled at us when our ball landed on his front yard.

Behind our houses were 45 acres of woods. The deed belonged to a church, but the woods belonged to 72 kids.

We knew just about every inch of those woods. We'd build forts and throw rocks and lift old logs, looking for salamanders, and build little dams on the tiny stream that was so deep in the woods that the little kids were afraid to go there.

Dogwood Terrace was my world, and it was safe. We could leave the house at 7:00 in the morning, go out and play or explore all day, and come home at 6:00 or 7:00 for dinner. At night we would run through the neighborhood, playing kick the can or freeze tag. Sometimes, in the summer, bats would swoop at the streetlights after bugs. The girls would scream and the boys would throw stones in the air to test their sonar. The only dangerous weapons in my childhood were Popsicle sticks we had sharpened on the sidewalk.

Ramsey was a lot like Bedford Falls in *It's a Wonderful Life*. The town had summer day camp in the park, Little League baseball, Pop Warner football, Boy Scouts, and field trips to museums and historical landmarks. George Bailey's family would have fit right in.

The public schools educated us well, and the church helped to teach us right from wrong. My parents' "community child-rearing plan" was going splendidly. Then we hit puberty.

The church taught us sex was dirty, and the schools didn't teach us much of anything at all.

## Sammy & Ellie: A Love Story

They called it Health, and it was taught for two days by my seventh-grade gym teacher, Mr. Groh. The boys whose hormones were awakening needed to be clued in about the changes taking place in their bodies. Mr. Groh closed off the geography room and covered the window to the hallway.

The vehicle he used to teach us about sex and reproduction was the compelling saga of Ellie Egg and Sammy Sperm. Complete with little cartoon charts. At one point, old Mr. Groh got his charts mixed up with the geography maps and Sammy sailed past the Cape of Good Hope on his way to the fallopian tube.

Mr. Groh told us about wet dreams but called them "nocturnal emissions," which was way too official sounding to me and evoked visions of a Senate subcommittee: "If you'll recall, Jim, in 1969 the Nocturnal Emission determined that Oswald acted alone." Mr. Groh taught us one thing about sexual intercourse that I will never forget. And I *quote*, "When you first get married, it takes about five minutes; but after you're married for a while, you can get it down to about 30 seconds." That is a true story.

**Nice guys finish last.**

## Original Sin: Now New and Improved!

Much of the ritual and ceremony of the Catholic Church is arcane, and the Church's openness on sex is no different. One of the few things I heard about sex from the Catholic Church is that masturbation is a sin. Nothing drives home lessons about a loving, God-given sexuality like fear and guilt. They called masturbation "self-abuse."

Masturbation is abuse, and boxing is a sport. This is one of the first instances I can recall where I began to doubt the authorities in my life. I have a great deal of experience with masturbation, and I can tell you I have never suffered a knockout. Not even technical. Sure, a couple of standing eights, but you have to expect that when you are in training. And train I did. I coulda been a contender.

According to the Church, I was born with original sin. They didn't want to allow me one second of innocence. "Welcome to the world. You are dirty."

One of the appeals of organized religion has always been its simplistic and authoritative answers for complicated issues. Even recently, church leaders have tried to blame teen sex on rock-and-roll music. Teenagers have sex for a lot of reasons. I don't think rock and roll is one of the reasons. If you're going to peg teen sex on rock and roll, why don't we just blame incest on country and western?

Without the schools and the church to teach us about sex, that left only *Playboy* magazine and Jimmy Kelly.

### "Wow! Jimmy Kelly Knows Everything!"

Jimmy Kelly learned sex on a street corner in Brooklyn and brought that street corner to Dogwood Terrace. I had never heard of a "hua" until I met Jimmy Kelly. When I was 12, I walked around saying "hua" for three months, without knowing what a "hua" was, because the cool new guy from Brooklyn was saying it.

You know, "*hua*"—"whore" with a Brooklyn accent.

My first kiss was when I was 13. Jimmy Kelly had brokered a little game of spin the bottle with my older sister's girlfriends. I was nervous and intrigued. I liked it.

Also when I was 13, my father caught me with a *Playboy*. Fortunately, I had both hands on it at the time. My older brother, Bob, was demonstrating to me the trick to hiding a *Playboy* inside a big book on the bookshelf when in walked my father.

My heart jumped, and I froze in fear. My father, a strict Catholic, reacted predictably. He said, "Get that out of my house! I will not have that crap in my home."

My brother is three years older than me and truly enjoyed watching me panic. After Dad left the room, Bob called him a "prude" and I agreed, and we both had a good laugh at the image of Pops getting all heated up about something as silly as naked pictures. But just a few short minutes earlier, I had thought surely God would strike me dead.

I didn't know it at the time, but this episode was my personal introduction to every man's lifelong process of reconciling his sex drive with his conscience. Pack a lunch; this could take a while.

■ ■ ■

I had a good idea that God did not want me looking at pictures of naked women. Although I'm sure He must have expected it, being as how He's the one who gifted me with original sin and all. He'd have to be a hypocritical God not to expect it. Anyway, I don't know how really "original" it is if everyone has it.

Just a few years ago, I asked my dad, "What was the deal with the way you reacted to that *Playboy*? I mean, there were other reactions you could have had that were a little less likely to induce baggage. How about 'Yeah, naked women, fellas. They're nice to look at; don't get carried away.' Why not something like that?"

He said, "God knows, I wasn't perfect. But back then, with Hugh Hefner and his 'Playboy Philosophy,' I knew what that was going to do to marriages and families, and to see it enter my home really upset me."

As I look back, I realize that growing up, I had one major flaw. I laughed at the people I should have listened to, and I listened to the people I should have laughed at.

# TWO
# QUESTIONS

## Bicentennial

**M**y sex life switched from the theoretical to actual on the Fourth of July, 1976. The country was 200 years old, and I was 18.

Shortly thereafter, I experienced my first extremely painful breakup. I think when puppy love ends—if you can call it puppy love at 18—that first big breakup hits you especially hard. You have no reference to understand that this kind of thing is going to happen over and over and over . . . *so get used to it.*

The initial separation knocks you for a loop. Makes you irrational. Here's something I did. Have you ever done this? Right after you break up with your first love—you're a teenager, you're on autopilot, and you're an idiot, basically—you don't even know why, you just drive by her house late at night and look over. . . .

As though she's going to come running out of the house at 2:30 in the morning and suddenly marry you.

"Hey! I changed my mind. Good thing you were driving by!"

I'm a little embarrassed to admit it, but I drove by my first girlfriend's house almost every night for a month. A lot of us did that. Of course, now it's called stalking.

I'm down to about once a week now. Her kids stand on the driveway and wave. I'm pretty sure she had the kids just to make me jealous.

**I was going to go to a codependency support group, but I couldn't get anyone to save me a seat.**

After the breakup, I experienced what I've come to know well as "aerobic crying." Crying so deep and extensive that you get a great cardiovascular workout going. You bury your head in the pillow so people three miles away can't hear.

They say pain is a wonderful source of motivation. I'd say the motivation comes more from the desire to avoid pain again at any cost.

To that end, I've spent much of my adult life trying to answer two questions. The first question is "What makes a man?" If I am first a man, then let me be good at that. If this is the machinery I'll be operating my whole life, let me familiarize myself with it, let me figure out the control panels. Hopefully I'll manage to get beyond that big toggle switch in the middle.

And the second question is, of course, "What do women want?" That's a good one.

**Any man who tells you
he understands women
is full of shit.**
**—JOHN AMATO**

## Sense of Humor

"Women want a man with a good sense of humor."

I've heard those words all my life, and all men hold them to be true. Some men hear it and make the mistake of thinking that it means women want you to tell them jokes. But that's not what a sense of humor is about. A sense of humor isn't "Two Jews walk into a bar. . . ."

A sense of humor is a sense of balance in your spirit. A sense of humor is a sense of proportion in your soul. It allows us to assign the right degree of importance to things that arise. It's a stance of objectivity within which we can instantly determine what's important and what is not. It's "right-sized thinking."

A sense of humor is important to women because women need to feel safe. A woman needs to know, for example, that if her husband's football team loses, he's not going to throw a beer bottle through the television. Because it's just not that important.

A man with a good sense of humor provides an environment where a woman can relax and trust that there will be no bonehead moves. He possesses a sense of discernment that will keep him from doing something painfully inappropriate that would cost the people around him. A good sense of humor leads to a sense of trust and security. Plus, it's just plain fun to be around.

Not only does a good sense of humor help us not take things too seriously, but a good sense of humor also lets us determine which things should be taken seriously.

And since a sense of humor is the tool that helps us discern what is appropriate, that's what makes it so extra cringeworthy when a man makes an inappropriate sexual

joke around women. I've seen guys make a lame, overly familiar sexual remark, and when a woman doesn't laugh,
they blame her for not having a sense of humor. "Jeez.
What's with you, anyway??"

I think I get my sense of humor from my father. My father is a wiseass. My father told me the reason we hide
Easter eggs is because Jesus had really high cholesterol
levels.

You'd think with all that fish in his diet . . .

When I was 12 years old, I was in my bedroom reading
the Bible. My father came in and said, "Hey, guess what.
Jesus dies in the end."

"Thanks for ruining it, Dad."

When I went to college, I majored in philosophy. I told
my father my plans, and he said, "Philosophy? Why don't
you minor in communications so you can wonder out
loud?"

I brought my college sweetheart home to meet my parents for the first time. She told my father her major was
women's studies. He said, "Gee. It must be hard memorizing
all those recipes."

I know. He was kidding. My dad could joke like that because we all knew it was the furthest thing from who he is.
With three daughters and a consistent decency to his character, my dad would say to my brother and me, "You respect
your sisters, you respect your mother, and you respect
women."

When my father spoke of the importance of showing
consideration toward others, you knew he believed it to be
an important part of being a man, and you believed it, too.
I rarely hear his voice and those of millions of principled

men like him represented in our popular culture. That's one of the reasons I set out to write this book.

My father is a gentleman. He told us, "A man is someone who loves women, loves children, loves the planet, and protects them."

My father is an idealist and a dreamer. He has spent a large part of his retired life working to design a specially contoured car seat for people who drive with their heads up their ass.

> Studies show that
> 90 percent of people think
> they are better-than-average drivers.
> Forty percent of them
> are wrong.

## "Nice Car. Did It Come with Turn Signals That Year?"

Everyone thinks they're a good driver. But not everyone is a good driver. There are a lot of bad drivers out there. I know because I have imaginary conversations in traffic with these people.

Likewise, many people think they are relationship experts. Everyone's got great advice for you. You can call a friend for advice, and she'll solve all your problems in 10 seconds. Never mind she's sleeping with a married ex-con heroin addict who has 14 children by 12 different mothers. . . . She'll gently help you understand you have "rescuing" issues to deal with.

It's easy to give others relationship advice, but when it comes to our own problems, we are strangely blind. A friend can call me with a long list of weighty problems, and I'll have all the answers instantly. Then I'll hang up the phone and spend 15 minutes trying to decide what shirt to wear.

I've never been real good at relationships. I'm getting better; I try to educate myself, you know. But for me, and for a lot of the people I know, I think part of the problem is generational. We grew up during the sexual revolution. I don't have a lot of relationship skills because all of my training is in casual sex. Check my résumé. My entire background is in casual sex. I know how to seduce; that's the easy part. I just never had a clue what to do *after* that.

I am, however, a very good driver.

# COMMUNICATION

Do you want to know why
communication is so important
to a relationship? Do you want to
know why? Actually, I don't really
feel like talking about it right now.
—COMEDIAN PAUL PROVENZA

**C**ommunication is the most important element in a relationship. Without communication, there is no relationship—you're just two people in the same room. Many men would sincerely tell you they believe sex is the most important element. But sex is communication. Good sex communicates all of the passion you can't put into words. And what an eloquent ineloquence it can be. Sex between two people can be an incredibly beautiful thing. Especially if you can get between the right two people.

I think women are naturally better at communicating their needs and emotions than men. Because they've been practicing for millions of years. Since the dawn of human history, women have been getting together with their friends and discussing men, striving to reach an understanding: "He did that? I don't believe it, that bastard. Then what did he do? You should leave him."

Men should think long and hard before doing something stupid around women. Women can be your best press or your worst nightmare.

I have one piece of advice for men: If you break up with a woman, you had better do it smoothly, or you will never get another good one again. Why? Women have an intelligence network that rivals the CIA. They make the Internet look like two tin cans with string tied between them. I guarantee, if you screw over a woman tonight, by tomorrow morning you'll be on a shit list in Afghanistan.

Women are constantly conferring with their advisers. They are basically researchers. Especially in bed. That only looks like a negligee; it's really a lab coat.

I'm a big fan of the negligee. For guys a negligee is considered "gift wrapping." That's why it usually has a little bow on it. "Ohhh. For me? You shouldn't have. I didn't get you anything."

Gift wrapping, incidentally, had to have been a woman's idea. If it had been a man's idea, we would just spray paint the box.

Men love lingerie because men are visually activated. That's what gets us going. We love to look. Women peak sexually at around 35. Men peek at anything we can.

I can't speak for all men, but that's why I like tan lines so much. There's a mystery to it. And men are drawn to mystery because mysteries beg to be solved. There's also the undeniable allure of exclusivity: "This never sees the light of day." Like freshly fallen untracked snow on a crisp winter morning.

When I see tan lines, I get a feeling much like what I imagine Henry Fonda's Tom Joad must have felt while feasting his eyes on the verdant San Joaquin Valley after that long and arduous trek from the dust bowl in *The Grapes of Wrath*. Haven. Hope. The promise of better days ahead.

Or I picture Lewis and Clark standing atop that mountain, witnessing for the first time the vast, awesome beauty of the Pacific Ocean as far as the eye can see. Lewis turned to Clark and said, "Beautiful, isn't it?" Practically overpowered by emotion, Clark managed to utter, "Like . . . tan lines."

Where was I? Oh, yeah. Men are visually stimulated. This helps give rise to the theory that women may be more evolved than men. It's a widely accepted notion that men get sexually excited by looking at the pictures, and women are more likely to be stimulated by erotic literature.

Now, parallel that to the evolution of an individual human life: We start out life looking at the pictures; then, when we are about five years old, we learn how to read. Perhaps that's where women left us behind. Right about there.

Women read erotic *li-tra-ture*. Guys look at dirty pitchurs.

Communication skills are tied to the desire to fulfill one's needs. It's very clear that men and women just have differing ideas on what it is we, and each other, seem to need. It's not that men completely lack communication skills. It's just that men's communication skills are more likely to be honed in areas where men's needs lie. Consequently, we've developed some seemingly peculiar communication abilities. Men can take any phrase in any language and instantly make it perverse.

> MAN 1 (pointing to a woman): You see that woman? She's got a 170 IQ, she's a Rhodes Scholar, she's a nuclear physicist. . . .
> MAN 2: Really? I'd like to nuke *her* physics.

Guys will assume that because you're another guy, you want to hear this level of conversation. Men love to talk to their friends about their sexual conquests. In fact, at one point I had considered writing a play called *The Penis Monologues*. Then I quickly realized that men telling stories about their penises isn't theater; it's just life. You don't have to hire a babysitter and call Ticketmaster to hear that.

In the early days of Man, our collective survival depended on individuals sharing their exploits upon their return from parts unknown. Men would come home from hunting trips and share their experience so the others could learn how to find what they needed while avoiding predators. These stories also helped position us in ranking amongst our fellows. So, sharing our experiences is bred into us. But now that we're a little more socialized and do most of our hunting with a shopping cart, it would be nice if we could show a little class. A little decorum.

I've always been uncomfortable listening to other guys brag about sex. It feels creepy. I always want to ask, "Which did you enjoy more, having sex with the woman or telling your friends about it afterward?" Describing to your friends in graphic detail the sex you've had with a woman is basically phone sex with your friends, without the phone.

I wish men were a little more aware of the damage they create when they talk about a woman behind her back. The damage I'm talking about, of course, is that women would be much more inclined to have sex with us if we would just shut the fuck up.

■ ■ ■

Even if a guy isn't having sex with a woman, he'll be happy to let you think it's happening. He may not lie outright, but he'll let you suppose he's having sex with her. Women go in the other direction.

A few years ago, I was writing a show for George Hamilton and his ex-wife Alana Stewart. We were in my office, and George was teasing Alana about the new man she was seeing.

Alana was protesting, "George, he's just a friend. I don't know why you're making such a big deal. He's just a friend."

George turned to me, smiling, "That's what women always say when you ask about 'that guy.' 'Oh, him? He's just a friend.' Then, a week later, you're in bed with her and he breaks down the door to prove his friendship.'"

. . .

Because women haven't the physical strength of men, they have needed to rely more on their verbal and argumentation skills to defend themselves. And the more experience they have with defending themselves, the better they are at it. I was walking past a house, and I heard a woman inside shout this at a man:

"You always do that! That's why your son is the way he is. I don't want to talk about it."

Let's step back for a moment to appreciate the sheer beauty and precision of that surgical strike.

Three sentences.

Three rules of debate broken.

Not a syllable wasted.

Masterful.

Lonely.

It's very difficult for a man to win an argument with a woman. Women have very effective arguing techniques. For example, if a woman senses she's losing the logic of an argument, she'll shift gears and argue about the way you're arguing just to throw you off.

You can physically feel the power of the argument leave your body as she glazes over like she's not listening. You get frustrated, maybe a little more aggressive. She throws up her arms and turns to walk away, saying, "Well, I'm not even going to deal with you if you're going to be like that."

That's the guilt tax we pay for being "man the oppressor." As soon as you raise your voice in frustration, you mimic a man who's bullied her in the past, and she becomes defensive. All she can do at that point is throw you off balance; so you redouble your efforts, throwing her even more into defense mode. You accelerate each other.

Here's an example of how guys can never be right in any given situation: You are with your girlfriend or your wife, whatever the case may be. She reminds you of something you did together maybe years earlier, and you don't remember it. Watch out.

She says, "Honey, you remember? Remember that?"

"Um . . . no."

"You jerk."

So, you are the bad guy. But what happens in the exact same situation when you ask her and she doesn't remember?

"Honey, remember the time we did that together?"

"No. That must have been *some other woman you were with.*"

■ ■ ■

Do you know that the smartest person in the world is a woman? She'll be happy to tell you. Her name is Marilyn vos Savant—because just in case you may not know that she's the smartest person in the world, she changed her name to the Latin words for basically "I am the smartest person in the world!"

And I have no reason to doubt her claims to that title. Even if I did doubt her, let's face it. She's the smartest person in the world—even if *one* of the smartest people in the world tried to convince you they were the smartest person in the world . . . well, you'd lose, wouldn't you? Because you are not as smart as they, are you? Stop wasting my time.

Anyway, it doesn't surprise me that the smartest person in the world is a woman.

And it shouldn't surprise you, either.

## Domestic Priorities

The smartest person in the world is a woman, and according to television, the dumbest person is every man on the planet. In the TV-commercial world, men cannot exist without the naturally smarter woman to set him straight about Ty-D-Bowl. "Thanks, honey! You're the greatest!"

Have you seen this commercial on TV? A man and a woman are on a dock, about to get on a boat for the day, and the guy pipes up, "What if my diarrhea comes back?"

I just wish the woman would say, "Deal with it! I will re-assure you when you're feeling down. Sometimes I'll even pick up your socks off the floor. I will run the family check-book. But when it comes to your bowels, I'm just not quite that codependent, got it? Damn. I married a child."

• • •

Couples get married, and more often than not, the woman runs the checkbook. If the guy runs the money, he's usually one of three things. An accountant, a banker, or an Italian guy saying, "What are you? Outta your friggin' mind?"

Usually the woman runs the money, and there's a good reason for that. It's because married men are formerly single men. Most single men will spend money on things other than taking care of themselves. We'll drink beer, play poker, but mostly we blow our money trying to impress women. There's a reason the Corvette is the longest-selling sports car in history.

When it comes to money, single guys do not have high domestic priorities. I know this firsthand. I've done my laundry in shampoo. Add a little conditioner in the rinse cycle, and you've got yourself some extremely manageable Van Heusens.

When I was single, I had nine lamps in my house. At one point, I waited till I got down to one bulb that I'd carry from room to room. And it would waste a lot of time because you gotta sit there in the dark, waiting for it to cool down. That's why men leave their socks lying around—we need them for oven mitts.

I am not the only man who would leave dirty socks and dirty clothes lying around. Women, however, leave piles of clean clothes. You tell me which of those phenomena makes more sense.

It's that pile that forms right before they go out at night. The "discards."

She's standing in front of a mirror: "I won't be wearing *that* tonight."

Then, she says (to the clothes), "You are hereby sentenced to remain in a wrinkled mass of shame, unworthy of my adornment."

Here's another great example of how single men will cut corners. I bought a set of dishes for the first time when I was 32. I had owned the bachelor cereal bowls before, but this time I left the store with eight place settings. Because I took a woman along with me to help me pick them out.

This should give you an idea of how women think differently than men. She said, "Definitely get eight place set-tings. . . . You'll want to entertain, you know, have people over for dinner."

What was *I* thinking? "Eight meals in a row without doing the dishes." Not including eating the cereal out of the coffee cups.

There is a reason other than laziness that men will leave dirty dishes lying in the sink. That pile of dishes is something familiar in an otherwise lonely, hostile, and unpredictable world. You are able to walk by and see piles of plates and bowls in the sink, and they are like that old friend you keep bumping into once in a while, saying, "We've got to get to-gether sometime." But you never do. Seriously, who's got time these days?

When I was younger and single, finding ways to avoid re-sponsibility was an art form. The challenge of resourceful-ness is always a wonderful source of satisfaction from accomplishment. My limited writing skills cannot convey to you the feeling of satisfaction I got the day I discovered that the rubber stopper for the sink disposal will perfectly seal a half can of cat food.

Go ahead. Check. I'll wait.

• • •

When I was single, I thoroughly enjoyed being irrespon-sible. That's one of the benefits of being single. You are ac-countable to no one. You're a "maverick." A "lone wolf." Or any number of romanticized labels one might use to justify irresponsible or antisocial behavior.

But while that mind-set works when you are single and accountable to no one, it doesn't prepare you for when the time comes to be responsible to someone else. It's important to recognize when the transition at hand calls for a change in attitude.

I've often heard guys complain that women are mercenary. Guys will say, "Women just want guys with money. What about my personality?"

I've got news for you: By the time you're 35, your personality should have some money.

It's not about the money, Stuey. It's about being able to take responsibility. If you can't take care of yourself, don't go complicating someone else's life.

But when Stuey and a bunch of his friends spend Saturday night drinking beer on his garbage-picked couch because they can't seem to get girlfriends, it's easy for them to agree that women are shallow and only interested in money. It's much easier to blame than to go deep down inside and discover how dark and hollow and empty you might be. Pride makes it hard to face your inadequacies. So you reflexively find fault in women. Especially when no one bothers to call you on it.

> **Faults are thick**
> **where love is thin.**
> **—ENGLISH PROVERB**

## Blame

Men blaming women isn't new. This goes all the way back to the Bible. Who wrote the Bible? Men. Notice how readily the Bible blames Eve for the all the problems of mankind.

"Eve tempted Adam with that apple and it was the birth of original sin."

I don't think it happened that way. I've been to night-clubs. Odds are Adam was hitting on her relentlessly. At first she was polite and gracious. Finally she got to the point where she said, "Would you just go away? I wouldn't sleep with you if you were the first man on earth."

That's when Adam became the very first man to try to guilt a woman for giving him "blue balls."

"You don't know what seeing you in that fig leaf does to me, Eve. Come on. I gave you a *rib*. And I get nothing? Just *touch* it. I won't tell anybody. There *isn't* anybody."

Finally she rolled her eyes and threw him a mercy lay. They had a kid, and the rest is history.

But they'll try to tell you that Adam was just minding his own business, you know, trying to have a beer and watch the game without being pestered. Because most of history was written by men.

The city of Chicago burned down in 1871. We are *still* blaming Mrs. O'Leary for that cow. I heard about it in sixth-grade history class.

"Where was Mr. O'Leary?" I blurted out.

There *was* a Mr. O'Leary. He was at the local tavern, hoisting a few cold ones. But I guess since Mrs. O'Leary had the privilege of waking up to milk the cow every morning at 5:30, it was *her* cow when Chicago burned down, wasn't it? I bet if that cow had pissed on the fire and saved Chicago, it would have been Mr. O'Leary's cow.

∎ ∎ ∎

**"Hey. Women blame men, too."**

Yeah. Women are screwed up. Men are screwed up. Men are assholes, and women are bitches. Conclusions like these mark the end of discussion and any possibility of happiness. The end of a willingness to believe that there might be something better.

If you think men are assholes or women are bitches, you're right. Live in your men-are-assholes-and-women-are-bitches world. When you're 90 years old, you can sit in a wheelchair in the corner of an old-folks home, and hopefully God will be kind enough to give you dementia so you won't recognize that you've lived three percent of your possibilities because of cynical labels.

Sure, women blame men. But all I can do is take care of my side of the street and have faith that it will have a favorable impact on the people around me. I can't change "her." Thank God I can look at my problems and be willing to change some things about myself because if I have to change "her" in order to feel okay with myself, I am in deep shit. Because it's never going to happen. All I can do is look at my part in things and try to come up with what I can bring to my relationships.

The men I admire don't blame others. They assess, and then they take responsibility. They think about what they can bring to a situation. Ignorant and incomplete men are quick to blame women. They will consistently go from zero to blame in 1.3 seconds, never learning that located in the area between zero and blame, you will find most of the skills and knowledge that make up a man's character.

# COMMITMENT

You are "pronounced" married.
There are only two times in your life
when you get "pronounced." You get
pronounced married and you get
pronounced dead. Somewhere there's a
cynic saying, "What's the difference?"

**My** friend Jerry just got engaged. He bought his fiancée that diamond ring because that's what men do when they propose. I thought I'd mess with him. I asked, "Why'd you buy her a diamond?"

"Well, you know, it's a tradition."

"Any idea how that tradition got started?"

"Absolutely *no* idea."

*I* know how that tradition got started: One man bought a woman a diamond and she told her friends. It's just that simple.

The next day this guy's friends are banging on his door. . . .

"Nice going, pal. Now we all gotta do that. Engagement *ring*, you say? How clever. 'Engagement boat' ever enter your mind? 'Engagement motorcycle'? 'Engagement season football tickets' would be a nice tradition."

When you think about it, whoever came up with the idea of combining diamonds and marriage must have been pretty smart. What better to symbolize marriage than the hardest thing known to mankind?

. . .

For one human being to love another:
That is perhaps the most difficult
of our tasks; the ultimate,
the last test and proof,
the work for which all other work
is but preparation.
—**RAINER MARIA RILKE**

When I was a teenager, I played pool on weekends with a 75-year-old man named Christopher Ryan. Chris was a gentleman. Old-school. A "dandy." He carried himself with a quiet dignity and class. On his left hand he wore a white cotton glove so his ebony cue stick could slide smoothly through his shots. He had won that stick in a tournament 50 years earlier. That was one of the few things I knew about his life. He never talked much about himself.

But I knew he loved his wife. I only met Mrs. Ryan once, after a big snowfall when I showed up at their house and, in a showy gesture of kindness, insisted they let me shovel their driveway for free. Afterward, she invited me in for hot cocoa. This was Bedford Falls, after all.

I was struck by the air of tenderness and gentility between the two of them. There are some elderly couples who, after 50 or 60 years, just give up fighting each other. They learn how to get along. It's a benign tolerance. But this was different. This man clearly admired this woman. This was a love that had endured and grown. I was 17 and completely self-absorbed, but when you see true love, you know it.

The only other time I went to the Ryans' home was about a year later. Chris had stopped showing up at the pool hall. I went to his house and found out Mrs. Ryan had died a few weeks earlier. He invited me in but had nothing to say. He looked like a man who had walked into a room and forgotten why. Our visit was awkward and uncomfortable. He set himself to explain, but no words came and he shook his head and I could tell he knew the words would never come.

A few months later he was in a convalescent home, withering away. With my whole life ahead of me, I was naïvely optimistic and trying to cheer him up. He fixed on my eyes and said quietly, "I have no reason." And suddenly I had perspective and I knew he was right, and I said goodbye and let him be.

I know there is a depth and great value to loving one person with all your heart. I saw it with the Ryans, and I've seen it many times since. Cynics don't talk about it. But I know it's possible.

### "Please Color within the Lines"

Have you ever been in a relationship where you suddenly realize, "This person would be having the exact same relationship whether I was here or not?"

They've got a script. Sometimes they've spent their entire life planning how everything is going to be when they find you. Whoever you are. And they're going to be *really good at it.*

I knew a comedian from Chicago who loved performing and loved playing golf. Stand-up comedian was the perfect job for him because he could play golf courses all over the country during the day and work at night.

He was performing at a club in Phoenix and met a woman and they fell in love. Soon they decided to get married. She told him he'd have to move to Phoenix because that's where her family was. So he did.

A few months into the marriage, she told him she didn't like his traveling all the time, so he'd have to stop doing stand-up and get a real job. So he quit stand-up and got a day job. At least he'd still have the weekends for golf.

A few months later, she told him that since he was at work all week, weekends were really the only time she got to see him, so he needed to stop playing golf. So he stopped playing golf. Six months later, she left him.

She said, "You're not the man I married."

• • •

When it comes to relationships, you can theorize all you want, but you don't really know until you're in it. We bite off more than we can chew, and then we chew really hard and really fast.

You can try to learn. You can read the books. Which is another reason I think women are better at relationships—because they have all those relationship books.

There are approximately four hundred thousand relationship books written for women, give or take a hundred thousand. Guys have two books. And one of them is called *How to Pick Up Chicks*. I haven't read it, but I'm guessing that the author's reference to women as "chicks" sets the foundation for some progressive insights.

You could take the higher road and read *Iron John*, the

bible for the 1980s men's drum-banging bonding movement. *Iron John* always sounded to me more like something
you'd sit on to *have* a men's movement. Don't forget to bring
along *How to Pick Up Chicks* so you'll have something to wipe
your ass with.

You know the women's books I'm talking about? *Women
Who Love Too Much. Smart Women/Foolish Choices. Women Who
Run with the Wolves. Women Are from Mars, Men Have a Penis.*
Have you read that one?

Obviously, it's *Men Are from Mars, Women Are from Venus*
written by John Gray. Have you seen this guy on television?
He's the Omega Male. On behalf of the people of Earth, I'd
like to invite John Gray to stop by and do a couple of
pushups.

Do you know who John Gray was married to and is now
long divorced from? Barbara De Angelis. Relationship author. Relationship expert. Relationship guru. Do you see
where this is heading?

Two of the premier relationship gurus in America were
married to each other, and *they* couldn't make it work. It's
like getting hairstyling tips from Nick Nolte's mug shot.

What was the deal with Nick Nolte giving *himself* a date-
rape drug? On the news they said, "Nick Nolte was pulled
over. His car was weaving all over the road in Malibu. Police
gave him a blood test, and they found Rohypnol in his system." Nick was high on *roofies*. I can only assume the day finally came where he had just had enough: "I am getting so
tired of buying myself flowers . . . taking myself out to
dinner . . . taking myself to the movies. You know what?
Tonight *I* get what *I* want."

Back to the matter at hand. The problem I have with some of these books is that they supply yet one more agenda for someone to take to a relationship. One more simplistic blueprint into which you cannot cram all the infinite subtleties, nuances, and possibilities of a vital relationship. Relationships are living, breathing, and changing organisms. All the theory in the world doesn't help because theory of how it ought to be too often leads to expectations, and it's the expectations that mess it up. It's your script and your agenda that cause the troubles. Relationships are not paint by number.

I can't find happiness by focusing on the differences between men and women. I need to focus on the similarities and appreciate the differences. Anything else is selfish and controlling. If I believe I am from Mars and you are from Venus, doesn't that rob you of the opportunity to show me a little something special about, perhaps, Jupiter?

"Saturn has nice rings, but you'll never see them; there is no room for you to participate outside of the preconceived notion John Gray and I have planned for us. I'll be disappointed when you inevitably fail to meet my expectations. Welcome to your new role as 'The Source of My Disappointment.' Can I get you a drink? You'll need it."

I can't fault John Gray's overall message. Men need to listen to women more. I'm all for that. But don't feed it to me in a high chair.

My friend Susan swears the subliminal appeal of soap operas is that the men in soap operas actually care what the women are talking about. Watch for it the next time. Every one of these guys listens like it's the most important thing he's ever heard: "Oh, honey, I can't believe Erica and Blake broke up. Of all people. They seemed so happy. You gotta let me know how this works out."

. . .

My all-time favorite relationship book has got to be *Women Who Love Too Much*. How self-congratulatory is that title?

"Hey, what seems to be your problem?"

"I have too much love. Way too much love. In fact, this much love carries with it a tremendous responsibility. *Stewardship*, if you will. I have so much love to give that it gets me into trouble."

"Really? You mean it's not like you just keep choosing the same kind of jerk over and over again?"

I was in a bookstore in Alabama. Actually, *the* bookstore in Alabama. I was in the relationship section, a woman was looking for a book, and the woman who worked there was helping her. I thought I'd be funny. I said, "Do you have a book called *Men Who Get Blamed by Women Who Think They Love Too Much*?"

This woman didn't miss a beat. She said, "I'm looking for a book called *Men's Feelings*. . . . I think it's in fiction."

# "WE MAY NEVER HAVE PARIS"

## Boxing, Bubble Baths, and Big Boys Crying

Okay, here's the deal: Men have feelings. We just don't know what they are until two weeks after we have them. We're on tape delay.

We have feelings. We just have trouble recognizing them. And when we do occasionally recognize a feeling, we will often cross the street to avoid it, as though it were someone we owe money to.

Feelings are awkward and uncomfortable. Always have been. Most of our lives we've been taught—wrongly, I believe—that feelings are feminine, and "Don't be like a girl." Many boys are taught early that "boys don't cry." And so we just bottle them up inside and end up beating the shit out of someone because that's more honorable.

Perhaps there's a problem with being brought up with an attitude like that.

For starters, the line between masculine and feminine is not that clear-cut.

Look at boxing. Now, boxing, that's a big, tough-guy's, masculine sport, right? What's the prize money called in a heavyweight championship match?

The "purse." Here we have the two biggest, meanest men in the world fighting over a *purse*.

And a belt. All the latest accessories. Let's throw in some hoop earrings, maybe some five-inch stilettos. . . .

"That belt had better go with my gloves, or I'm not even getting in the ring."

I know guys who won't take bubble baths because they think it's not masculine.

I take bubble baths all the time. I love bubble baths—hell with it—I *cry* in a bubble bath.

Bubble baths are fun, they're peaceful and relaxing, they feel great—there's really no downside to taking a bubble bath. But there are a lot of guys who won't take bubble baths because they think "it's for girls." In fact, I'm told that it is because so many men think this way that the test marketing of "Mrs. Bubble" was such a miserable failure.

## "No Dove's Gonna Look at Me That Way and Get Away with It!"

A man's fear of appearing feminine can create a need to overcompensate that borders on the pathological. I was in Denver, and I saw a full-page newspaper ad for a sporting goods store. They were having a sale on shotguns. The banner in the ad read, "Dove Hunter's Special."

*Dove hunting is a sport.*

How small does your dick have to be before you actively hunt down and murder the *international symbol of peace*? If you're that hell-bent on irony, why not just march into the lobby of the U.N. and start stabbing people with a sharpened olive branch?

At least when it's a deer, it's almost your size. You drag it two miles through the woods, heave it up onto the hood of your car, and lash it down. What do you do with a dove? *Clip it to your visor?*

"What do you have planned for tomorrow, Jimmy?"

"First I'm going to wake up and have a bald eagle omelet.

"Then I'm gonna kick a panda in the nuts because they make me feel all weird inside when I think they're cute. I'm figgerin' on some spotted owl for dinner. 'Original'; not 'extra crispy.'"

. . .

"Don't be like a girl," we were told by gym teachers and coaches. The worst insult a boy could get in gym class was "You do that just like a girl." "You throw just like a girl. You tackle just like a girl." Or the coup de grâce: "You fight like a girl."

Whoever would have guessed that now, as adults, one of the best compliments a man can get from a woman is when she says during oral sex, "Wow, you do that just like a girl."

True story.

And speaking of oral sex—don't you think they should make beds about three feet longer so your legs don't dangle off the end of the bed? Or make your knees bend the other way or something. . . . I've been looking for a bed with leaves that fold out like a dining room table.

In addition to the culturally driven lack of experience we have in recognizing and heeding our feelings, we also have an underdeveloped ability to express them. And if you'd like to see a physical display of how well men express their feelings, all you need to do is watch a man on the dance floor. That's a perfect example of the difference between men and women. Women will lose inhibitions on a dance floor. It's something primal—deep in their DNA. On the dance floor, Mildred the librarian turns into Tina Turner. Men, on the other hand, are much more reserved and self-conscious. There's no way a guy can dance and raise his arms higher than his head without feeling gay. Can't do it. You hit that line just above shoulder level, and you may as well just go throw your hands into the sky in wild abandon. It's the "International Gay Line."

(That observation, by the way, was expressed on stage in

San Francisco almost nightly for three years. It's been thoroughly field-tested for political correctness. It is objective and completely nonjudgmental. Feel free to enjoy it without guilt.)

My last girlfriend loved to dance. She was a marathon runner. Stamina? Uh-huh. She used to say, "You know, you should talk a little more in bed; I kind of like that. Why don't you talk a little more during sex?"

And I wanted her to be happy so, reaching out my hand in desperation, I said, "*Water . . . water. . . .*"

### "No One Sees the Wizard!"

I tried everything I could think of to avoid my feelings for a long time. But there comes a point in a man's life when he has no choice but to listen to his feelings. That point is when the struggle to avoid feelings becomes more painful than the prospect of facing them. A man once told me, "Don't worry about getting in touch with your feelings; your feelings will get in touch with you."

The problem is, we don't learn how to face our feelings little by little when they first come up, so we don't build healthy coping skills along the way. When you finally get to a point where you do face your feelings, you need to break through maybe a 15- or 20-year accumulation of uncomfortable feelings that hit you all at once. Blam. Trust me. They're in there. And the only tools you have to deal with them are the same underdeveloped coping skills that told you to run from those feelings when they were small. Remember *Raiders of the Lost Ark* when they opened the Ark of the Covenant? All the ghosts started flying out and people's skin started melting off their faces and there were electrical storms and spirits swirling around? It feels a lot like that looks.

## Our Feelings, Their Ammo

We believe that as men we are supposed to be strong. While women see vulnerability as openness and an acceptance of truth, men often see no difference between vulnerability and weakness. In war and sports, vulnerability means a weakness in your defense. You are vulnerable to attack. It's survival of the fittest, and weakness is a fatal flaw. You never tell the enemy, "By the way, there's another door in the back of the fort that's always unlocked."

Men are terrified that women will turn our vulnerabilities against us. We're afraid our weaknesses are being filed away somewhere for the express purpose of making a surprise appearance somewhere down the road to bite us in the ass.

Consequently, the prospect of revealing our vulnerabilities to a woman initially seems to have very little appeal. At first glance, the risk-versus-reward ratio seems to lean heavily against us. We are afraid to share our feelings because we have a real good sense that we are inept at it. Inept isn't strong. The process of facing and moving beyond our weaknesses is an ordeal, and it's not the kind of thing you want someone to witness. Especially when the witness is precisely the person you'd like to impress the most. There's something to be said for appearing to be the strong, silent type. It's safe.

Vulnerability takes tremendous strength. The difference

between vulnerability and weakness lies in a man's willingness to take responsibility. Vulnerability doesn't burden the woman with an expectation to kiss it and make it better. Weakness does.

I've heard guys say, "Sure, women *say* they want us to be vulnerable, but when we *are* vulnerable, they want nothing to do with us."

There's a difference between a guy sharing a few intimate thoughts and his dumping a truckload of insecurities on her. Being that he's so new at opening up, it's possible that once the floodgates open, he'll pour out everything he's got to the point of collapse:

". . . and I'm getting kicked out of my apartment, and in second grade I peed myself at a spelling bee, and I hate music, and I like to dress in women's clothes, and sometimes I can't poop for three days, and last year I had a restraining order but she's a bitch and fucking lied, and I write to Britney Spears every day, and I'm afraid of mimes. . . . Hey! Where you going? I'm being *vulnerable* here!"

She asked *me* to open up, and then *she* shut down. Jesus. Women are schizo.

. . .

Eventually you have no choice but to lay yourself open and risk appearing weak. Eventually you'll meet someone you want to share your feelings with. And you'll trust her. And you'll know that the time has come where you have to share your feelings. Because that's what intimacy is about, sharing yourself. . . .

She wants you to open up to her. She says, "Talk about your feelings."

"Oh, man. If I was reluctant to share my feelings before because I'd lose power, you can bet your ass I'm going to be reluctant to share my feelings about my inability to get in touch with my feelings. I didn't want to face this alone every other time it's come up, and now you expect me to reveal all my weaknesses in front of you?

"All my life, to some extent, I've blown smoke and fire up against a huge screen—'I am the great and powerful Oz!'

"And now, for you, you'd like me to admit I'm just a little guy behind a curtain with a dog pulling at my pant leg? You want to cut Samson's hair, and you want to use Samson's scissors to do it? You want me to hang myself, and you want me to build the gallows? You want me to keep coming up with metaphors to distract you till you forget the issue?"

But you love her, you trust her, and the time has come to open up.

She says, "Talk about your feelings."

"Well, I think—"

"No, no, no. I know how you *think*; tell me how you *feel*."

And you love her, so you reach deep down inside. . . .

"I feel . . . like . . . *not talking*."

There! You did it!

**By the way, "I'd like to have sex with you and your best friend" isn't a feeling. It's a mistake. (And you really couldn't pick a worse time to bring that up.)**

## City of Lights

Young men have very little experience with, or even tolerance for, their feminine traits. We operated less on intuition and more on determination and aggression. I never learned nurturing as a boy. What's basically our experience as young boys growing up? We go out and play all day, and when we come home, Mom's got soup. We *get* nurtured.

Every once in a while, you'll see an excellent young man from a single-parent family. He knows Mom's got two jobs, and if he doesn't rub her feet tonight, she's never going to make it through her waitressing job tomorrow night. But he's an exception.

Because where do boys learn? Where do boys learn about relating to girls? *They learn from the accepted norm.* They learn from their peers. They learn from the local Jimmy Kellys; other guys their age—13, 14, 15—who haven't got a clue either. Or they learn from pornography. Not much nurturing there.

Much of what we've learned has been inadequate or completely based on ignorance, and now, with the proliferation of modern pornography, the ignorance has become aggressively mean-spirited.

Traditionally, young men haven't understood much about women, and that ignorance is now compounded by the fact that there's a whole generation of boys being "educated" on Internet porn and ugly, sad porn videos. For many young men, these are the only models of sexual behavior they know. Because adult males have abdicated their responsibility to represent alternatives.

When my father told me "No *Playboy*" when I was a kid, it was really no loss. Betty and Veronica from my sister's

Archie comics were enough to get me going. Mark Eden Bust Developer ads in the back of Mom's *Cosmopolitan* could do the trick.

But compared with the *Playboy* magazine of my youth, the porno of today is like mainlining heroin. Over the past 10 years, porn videos have become increasingly filled with degradation and assault. If you're worried that violent video games are teaching boys amoral aggression, go rent a Max Hardcore tape at your local mom-and-pop video store. Plop it in your VCR and consider that model of social inter-action getting staple-gunned to an impressionable young boy's sexual psychology. Kids are trading these tapes like baseball cards.

I don't believe in censorship. Men have a choice to give themselves and the women in their lives something better than this. No doubt sometimes it's about good, old-fashioned, pedal-to-the-floor fucking. But other times it's about sex as a gentle and passionate expression of your hu-manity. It's about recognizing your soul and honoring her soul and bringing them together.

But how easy is that choice to make if everything we are taught and everything we see and hear reinforces precisely the things that block us from experiencing true intimacy and loving, nurturing exchange? At a time when alienation in society has never been so strong, when human connec-tion is needed most, a primary means of human connection is becoming the most impersonal it has ever been.

If mimicking the behaviors in porno movies is all you have in your sexual repertoire, you are sexually retarded. If you think only of the physical, you're like a painter using one color. You can go to Paris and see the Louvre, and Notre

Dame, and the Left Bank, and the Arc de Triomphe; or you can go to Paris and hang out in the lobby of your Holiday Inn for two weeks.

If you're going to *go* to Paris, *see* Paris. Taste the food, meet the people, go to museums, and marvel at the architecture. Discover Paris. The postcards are pretty, but there's nothing like actually being there. And bring someone along with you. Paris is unbelievably romantic.

> **Men watch porn because it's fun,**
> **it's convenient, and because**
> **sometimes it's the only thing**
> **that will stop the pain of**
> **the emptiness it creates.**

### "Greetings from Asbury Park!"

It's my nature as a man to be driven by imagery. I can't change my nature. But I can temper my behaviors with a sense of deeper value I know in my heart. I need to accept that I am driven by imagery, and then show a little decorum around that. One doesn't want to be the human equivalent of the dog that humps somebody's leg every time company comes over.

I had an experience about 10 years ago that really put my relationship with pornography into perspective. Let me preface this by saying I've always liked and admired Bruce Springsteen. He's an artist and a poet who lives his life with tremendous passion and spirit. He has shared his gifts and given joy and added meaning to the lives of countless others. He is a man, in my eyes, who has tremendous dignity. He's "The Boss." If you doubt his impact on the world, consider this: The man single-handedly got the entire country to like *New Jersey*.

I live in Los Angeles and I was at 20/20 Video up on Sunset Boulevard, and I was going to rent a couple of porno movies. As I came out of the "adult" section with two movies, I headed for the checkout counter and realized that I was approaching at the same rate of speed and from the same distance as Bruce Springsteen and his wife, who were coming from the PG section of the store. I stopped dead in my tracks.

This moment, filled with equal parts embarrassment and fear, really put things in perspective. The contrast between our two lives was crystal clear and undeniable: He's "The Boss"; I'm "Eddy, the janitor who whacks off in the broom closet."

I pictured his next album coming out with the quintessential American folk ballad about the loneliness in the masturbator's eyes: The sound of an acoustic guitar rises up . . . a haunting, almost plaintive voice emerges from under the rhythmic bass guitar. . . . "He's got a hand full of lotion . . . and a mind fulla smut. . . . If only real life could be fast-forwarded to the good parts. . . ."

"Hey, Bruce, I saw you at the Meadowlands in '86. It blew me away."

"Yeah? Let me know how *Sex-Crazed Coeds* turns out."

# POTTERSVILLE

> Please help me.
> Something terrible's
> happened to me.
> I don't know what it is.
> Something's happened
> to everybody.
> **—JIMMY STEWART,**
> in It's a Wonderful Life

**R**icki Lake once had a 14-year-old girl on her show who wanted to have a threesome. Ricki was incredulous. Ricki said, "I can't believe it. You're 14 years old and you want to have a threesome. I mean, when I was 14, I was in Girl Scouts. Hell, I was still playing with dolls when I was 14—you want to have a *threesome*. Where do you *get* these ideas?" I was just praying this little girl was going to say, "From *you*. Every day I come home from school, I turn on the TV and witness social septicemia oozing from your show. Don't play naïve with me, PETA girl."

Not that a 14-year-old girl would use a phrase describing invasion of the bloodstream by virulent microorganisms from a focus of infection. But I would. Ricki Lake has no problem parading a long line of "bitches" and "hoes" and "hoochie mamas" across her stage for public humiliation. There's no ethical dilemma there. As long as they're not wearing fur—then we have a problem.

All of those shows . . . Jenny Jones, Maury Povich . . . Could Maury Povich have any more variations of the "My

Teenage Girl Is Out of Control" theme? Wasn't there some time back when he was actually a journalist, by the way? Did Connie Chung know she was marrying a carnival barker?

With shows like these, plus "Girls Gone Wild" ads on TV, Internet and video porn, 10 strip joints in every city . . . would it be at all possible for us as a society to suck any more of the dignity out of human sexuality?

How did we end up living in Pottersville? Remember *It's a Wonderful Life*? I feel like I'm in George Bailey's nightmare: I'm running panic-stricken down Main Street in Pottersville, yelling, "What's going on here? Where's Mary??"

"You're not gonna like it, George. Mary's humping laps in a strip joint."

Actually, they aren't called strip joints anymore. They are "gentlemen's clubs."

There's not a hint of irony in that, by the way. It's not tongue-in-cheek—like Robin Hood calling the biggest guy in his Band of Merry Men "Little John." You know, *gentlemen* . . . like they suddenly transform into David Niven in a smoking jacket when they stick a five-dollar bill in a stripper's G-string.

FYI, they're not strippers anymore. They're "dancers." And strictly speaking, they are dancers. And some of them are very good dancers.

However, I'm looking at the change in connotation that's occurred in our culture. I can only imagine how the classically trained dancer or ballerina feels about this association through shared job title.

Every time she meets a guy, she says, "I'm a dancer."

He says, "Oh, really? Uh, like, where at? Star Strip, Body Shop, Déjà Vu, Scores?"

"No, Lincoln Center, moron."

"Hey, wow. How much for a lap dance there? I hear that's a fuckin' classy joint, Lincoln Center."

Don't get me wrong here—I'm a big fan of naked women. It's just when they're turned into a form of commerce that my concern rises. I know I'm bucking a trend, but strip clubs make me sad. I feel the same way I feel when I walk into a pet shop; I can't stand seeing them in captivity. "Look. She's cold. Put a blanket on her. She's shivering."

"Uh . . . actually . . . I think that's the one on meth."

I'm pretty sure they call them "gentlemen's clubs" because "Place Where Guys Go to Perpetuate Abuse against Women Who Were Sexualized Too Young by Relatives and Neighbors" won't quite fit on the sign.

> **Sexual freedom has enslaved us.**
> **(My father was right.)**
>
> **. . .**
>
> **Whoso would be a man**
> **must be a nonconformist.**
> **—RALPH WALDO EMERSON**

I am 44 years old and have yet to name my penis. I think I'm going to go the distance. I have, however, named my love handles "Ben" and "Jerry."

Many men name their penis and it seems rather innocent,

even endearing, at first glance. Guys, if you want to name your penis, go right ahead. You know, be creative. Gladiator, Mister Big, Vesuvius—whatever. Search through history, television, and movies for just the right penis name. But be careful you don't choose a name the other penises will make fun of in the school yard. Penises can be very cruel.

To me, my penis is not a separate entity. I have chosen to view it as just another part of me. Some might think me prudish or uptight. Others may see my refusal to name my penis as selfish and ungrateful, as though it doesn't pay sufficient honor to one who has played such an important role in my life. Like not thanking your wife at the Oscars.

But I have several practical reasons for not naming my penis. First, I am aware that as soon as you name something, you run the risk of becoming way too attached to it. And frankly, I'm about as fond of my penis as a fella could possibly be. Anything more, and the next thing you know, I'm dressing it up in cute little outfits and hand puppets. "Look, everybody! It's Napoleon! Me and Napoleon are putting on a little show to raise money for new uniforms for the football squad! Then we're headed down to Sears Portrait Gallery for a few keepsake shots."

Second, from naming your dick and dressing it up, it's just a very short step to doing *really* ridiculous things. Things like blaming your dick for your behavior. "Ooops, I guess I was thinking with my dick!"

The idea of blaming your dick quickly becomes absurd if you extrapolate the logic. A penis has no cognitive awareness, no motivation, therefore no culpability. On its own it has no initiative. If you could blame your dick, it would follow that you could cross-examine your dick. Hey, while you're at it, why not scold your dick? "Bad dick! Bad penis! I can't believe I even hang around with you anymore."

But you have to stop short of blaming your dick for your problems.

If you are caught with your hand in the cookie jar, you don't blame your hand. Blaming your dick is a cop-out. If you choose to respond to your sexual urges with a selfish indulgence that will hurt someone, well, that's not "thinking with your dick"; that's just not thinking at all.

It sure would be nice if you could blame your penis. But then you wouldn't be able to see the real problem. You.

## Men Cheat

Guys will immediately respond, "Well, what about women? Women cheat, too."

Yeah. Women cheat. But generally when a woman cheats, it's because she realizes that no matter what she does or how hard she tries, she will never get what she needs from the relationship she's in, so she ends it through catastrophic intervention.

So, yeah, women cheat, too. But guys cheat *preemptively*. We cheat when things are going *well*. And if you ask us why, we have no answer. Or perhaps I was just thinking with my dick.

Admittedly, in many respects the sex drive in men can often be more powerful than the intelligence. I know this because I can be reading a book and stop at any time to have sex. I have never been in the middle of sex and said, "I gotta go catch up on *Anna Karenina*."

And I don't expect I ever will.

Unchecked, our sex drives will lead us to absurd decisions

and actions. I asked a guy I know why he cheated on his fiancée. The remorse was tearing him apart inside. He said, "It's hard to describe. I really wanted a committed relationship. . . . Well, a *part* of me really wanted a committed relationship. But apparently another part of me really wanted to put another part of me in a part of another woman. . . ."

But that's just part of it.

When a man's sex drive kicks in, it is accompanied by a bad combination of euphoric recall and selective memory. It exaggerates the promise of reward and won't call to mind the problems it might create.

Women seem to be perplexed by one question: "Why don't men want to commit?" Because we want to have sex with every woman there is. How hard is that?

I look at it like we have broken "wanting mechanisms." The part inside of us that wants what we want will too often control our decisions and actions. And we just want *more*. Gotta get it. Gotta have it. Gotta show it to you. The drive for acquisition is a prehistoric mechanism that serves our appetites, but often at the price of our greater needs. Because sometimes wanting "more" means hurting the people around you. Here's what I believe is a fundamental difference between men and women: A woman will meet a man and fall in love with him and think to herself, "I love this man."

A man in the same situation will think to himself, "If I can get *her* . . . well, just *think* of the possibilities. . . ." Part of it is conditioning. All of our lives, men's magazines have sold us the fantasy that we can have sex with the perfect woman. Women will look in the mirror and pick themselves apart for an imaginary five extra pounds. A man can be a homely

300 pounds, look in the mirror, and think he has a shot at the same women that want Brad Pitt. He deserves it. It's Miller Time.

We don't want to commit because we have vacationed in a sexual fantasy world our whole life. We're afraid that when we're in the church, standing at the altar, and saying, "I do," it will immediately be followed by Heidi Klum running into the vestibule, screaming, "Am I too late??!!"

I am not exaggerating. Such is the proliferation and power of our "Fantasy Guidance System." The FGS. Located in the brain. Clear across town from rational thought.

## Fisher Stevens Syndrome

Do you know who Fisher Stevens is? Probably not. He's an ordinary actor with unremarkable success. He's kind of a goofy-looking guy. He's not the kind of guy you would look at and think "ladies' man." Unless you were Fisher Stevens.

Fisher Stevens is probably best known for having dated Michelle Pfeiffer for several years in the early 1990s. In interviews Michelle gave and in articles written about her at the time, people would wonder what she saw in a goofy guy like Fisher Stevens, and she would say, "He makes me laugh. We have fun together. I love being with him."

Let me repeat because this is important: Fisher Stevens was dating Michelle Pfeiffer.

Well, one fine day Fisher Stevens was away on location, making a movie, when he allegedly cheated on Michelle Pfeiffer with an 18-year-old Woolworth's checkout girl.

Let that sink in. I'm guessing Fisher has by now.

I completely understand this. You see, sometimes, for some men, the constant stress of maintaining a level of intelligence becomes overwhelmingly difficult. The thinking goes a little something like this:

"On the one hand I have Michelle Pfeiffer. That is some world-class talent. Wow. I am in the big leagues now, baby."

Pause to think. Think *hard*. Think *really hard*.

"But she's not here.

"On the other hand, the girl ringing up my Cheetos looks very hot in that Mötley Crüe T-shirt. Watch and learn as I work my special magic."

Now, I don't know Michelle Pfeiffer. And obviously the knee-jerk reaction for most people looking at this would be to think, "Oh, my God, *Michelle Pfeiffer*. Is he *nuts*?" So I wanted to make sure I thought this through. She might be kind of hard to get along with. It's possible she has some bad habits. But this isn't about Michelle Pfeiffer. And it isn't about the girl at the checkout counter. It's about how little thought someone can give to something as important as trust.

Or no thought at all. Allegedly.

Fisher Stevens broke the trust. Michelle Pfeiffer dumped him. And Michelle Pfeiffer has moved on and seems to have a happy life. Last I checked, Fisher Stevens was sitting on his couch, eating a bag of Cheetos with his fingers crossed, hoping against hope that he might wangle an invite to Corey Feldman's 40th birthday party.

I'm pretty sure the relationship with the checkout girl didn't work out either.

**Pfisher Pfucked up. Allegedly.**

## Trust

Trust is the foundation of all good relationships. Trust is dropping your defenses. That's what you hand someone when you open your heart to them. "Here. Here's my trust. Don't hurt me." The worst ones will drop-kick your heart like a football and then blame you for the arc of the trajectory.

The sheer supply-and-demand ratio tells us how valuable trust is. Trust seems to be in very short supply these days. It's hard enough to feel safe in this world without having to doubt the one person who's supposed to love you. I see some men who treat marriage and commitment as though they're signing up for HBO; like it's just another entertainment choice. "I'll have Showtime, Cinemax, and a hooker. Just don't tell my wife, tee hee hee snicker snort."

There's a whole breed of these guys. When I travel, I see them in hotel lounges all across the country, laughing and thinking they're cute while working their unique brand of charm on cocktail waitresses with sore feet and little patience for assholes who think they're charming.

The waitress knows all about these guys because she had a husband who left her with three kids and a waitress job to support them. She knows deep in her wounded heart that a man who is led by his appetites is less man and more liability. But still she smiles. Because underneath this scene of married men living double lives in their imaginary world, a courteous smile means she might be able to buy new shoes for her children, who live in the only world that matters, mercifully far from the dirty, drunken whimsy of traveling liars.

**Kids, I'll be right with you.**
**Mommy needs a shower.**

## Liar

**Mr. Corleone is a man
who likes to hear bad news
right away.**
**—FROM THE GODFATHER**

I learned the hard way how important trust is. It's not really the kind of lesson you set out to learn. No one wants to go through the pain it takes to tattoo the trust lesson onto your ass.

Ten years ago I met a woman, Linda, and we seriously hit it off. Mental, emotional, spiritual, physical, almost a psychic connection. About two months into our relationship, I went out on the road and I met another woman and I slept with her. For one night. Told myself it didn't happen. The lies had begun.

Afterward, I rationalized that this had nothing to do with Linda; it was about me. It was something I needed to go through to put closure on my single life. I told myself that if Linda and I were to be together for the rest of our lives, well, the first two months were nothing compared with that. Besides, we hadn't really defined our relationship. . . . I mean, we never actually said we were exclusive. . . . Anyway, it would be better for her if she didn't know.

I chose to try to ignore the truth. I now believe it is a spiritual law that anytime you consciously make a decision to ignore a truth in your life, you no longer have any control over how many other truths that process will then choose to avoid on its own. Please keep your hands inside the ride.

I returned to town, and she sensed something had happened. She knew it. She asked if something had happened while I was away. And I did the worst thing a guy can do in that situation.

I denied it. I lied.

The truth was I wanted to avoid the consequences of my actions and I didn't have the integrity to call myself on my own bullshit.

Knowing what I know now, I fully understand the cruelty of that lie. With that lie, I had put her in a place inside of herself where she had to battle between her need to trust and her intuition.

It's a horribly mean and selfish thing to do to someone. How arrogant to think that I had any idea of what I was fucking with—or any right—when I fucked with that place.

Because that's where her joy lives.

That's where her smiles come from.

That's her soul.

Me, who had fancied himself the protector. Mr. Knight in Shining Armor who had spent his life believing that men should be strong and defend women.

Here is the hardest lesson I have ever learned: If you believe that a man should protect a woman, first and foremost protect her from *you*.

. . .

A month passed. We went to Hawaii for a week. We rented a beautiful little bungalow right on the beach in Kauai. Kauai is incredibly romantic—which makes it all the more painfully obvious when a romance is dead. The wall between us had become so thick that I had to admit what I had done.

I finally said, "What you thought happened did happen. I did it."

After that we took a stab at trying to work things out. But I had lied to protect my ass and in so doing sat by and watched her insides grind. My character had shown itself. And soon she left me. She told me, "You don't have the kind of awareness of yourself for me to feel safe, and I can't be around that."

The worst part was that I had to agree with her. I was standing face-to-face with my ignorance, and I knew it. It shook me to the core of who I was, and I saw that the core of who I was wasn't there.

There comes a time in a man's life where, up until then, you have done the best you could with the information you had. Before this, I was relatively hapless and naïve. I considered myself decent and harmless. But the difference here was that now my not knowing was hurting other people.

There's a point where naïveté becomes ignorance. And if you choose to avoid your ignorance when it reveals itself to you, it becomes arrogance to protect itself from being discovered. Arrogance will bully others to divert them from the truth.

I was at a crossroads. I could either face the truth of my ignorance, and take responsibility for it, or spend the rest of my life trying to contrive smoke and mirrors to keep people from seeing it. And frankly, I was beaten and lacked the energy for the second option.

The pain had kicked my ass into surrendering to becoming teachable.

**Dear Diary. Get awareness.**
**Whatever the hell that is.**

**7**

# WILLINGNESS

## Who's Driving?

**M**ost of my significant relationships have begun and ended in exactly the same place. When I'd meet a woman, I'd call up a friend: "I think she could be the one. We really hit it off. We spent the entire weekend in bed."

Then, when it ended, I'd be back on the phone: "It's over. I'm so depressed. I spent the entire weekend in bed."

But this breakup with Linda was the gut-wrenching worst. First, I went through about three weeks of aerobic crying. There's nothing like three weeks of intermittent sobbing to clean out the cobwebs.

Some of my friends tried to comfort me, to little avail. Their intentions were nice, but platitudes are never as trite and banal as when they apply. They'd say something like "Oh, don't worry. When you're in pain, it means you're growing."

Yeah. Like a weed through cement.

Or they'd say, "You're better off without her."

"No, actually I think she's better off without me. But anyway, thanks for stopping by with the morphine."

One friend suggested I should start looking at the patterns in my life, so I began keeping a journal. Incidentally, have you seen how much blank books cost lately? $11.95. How'd you like to be the author whose book is selling for $3.95? And they're *still* not moving?

You've just dedicated three years of your life and you've cut the value by two-thirds. . . .

So I started keeping a journal, and I also made a decision not to get involved with anyone for a while. That was a no-brainer. Since I was aware that I didn't have the goods, I knew any seduction would be dishonest. Seduction left my options column.

I realized that I had to become more than the sum of my appetites. I had to learn what drives me. Does my sex drive control me, or do I control my sex drive? If my unbridled and haplessly ungoverned sexual appetite had created wreckage, I had to find out what was on the other side of my sexual urges.

I made a decision to become chaste. Celibate. No sex. No masturbation. Because, I thought, if I've been masturbating since I was 12 or 13 every time I get the urge—you know, when I'm not in public—if I've been responding to that urge every time—almost every time—I get the urge and it's convenient, what's on the other side of that? What's on the other side of that wall? Maybe there's something to be learned.

I opened myself up to the possibilities that lay on the other side of my limited and limiting patterns. Maybe if I put aside the urge, I would get stronger. So that's what I did. No masturbation.

I made it 30 days.

Women chuckle, and guys say, "Jesus. How did you *do* that?"

I'm not sure. But I *can* tell you why I didn't make it to 31. At 30 days I met a woman and we went out for coffee and I started to explain this quest I was on. I explained how I was trying to follow a spiritual path to learn more about myself and get in touch with my drives, and to try to better understand the forces that drive my sexuality. I told her I wanted to truly discern between what was selfish and what was giving. . . .

And she was so impressed to meet a man who seemed to be so in touch with his feelings that she seduced me.

So I learned my first lesson in my newfound quest for spiritual awareness: "Wow! Celibacy is a great way to get laid!"

Once you step outside of a pattern, you can see how prevalent it is in your life. I could see how my sex drive shaped a lot of my decisions. I began to see just how much I am driven by sex. From how I decide what to wear, to how it drives my accomplishments, the places I go, what catches my eyes, and where my thoughts run to—so much of what I do is motivated by sex.

The other thing I found out at that point is that if you surrender to being teachable, teachers will enter your life.


### "Wow! Jimmy Kelly Knew Nothing!"

Shortly after Linda and I broke up, I needed a place to live. On a sunny morning I drove my motorcycle up into Laurel Canyon, looking for signs for guesthouse rentals. I got to the very top of the hill, and I looked to my right and saw a beautiful woman tending her roses. I almost didn't stop because I didn't want to break in on her reverie. But something told me it would be okay.

I said, "Excuse me. You wouldn't happen to know of any guesthouses for rent?"

She turned and sized me up for a long few moments.

"Well, I've been thinking about renting mine. Why don't you take a look?"

She opened the front gate, and beyond it was Shangri-la. Bougainvillea and rosebushes, flowers and a lemon tree. Everything was full of life and full of having been nurtured with feminine energy. There was a step bridge with a stream running under it, and two little ponds. The front door of the cottage was made in Holland in the 1600s, and everything in the house had a beautifully appointed feminine touch.

It was enchanted. If the Keebler Elves weren't gay, this is where their girlfriends would live.

A new world was presenting itself. I was turning the corner from the life I had fucked up to the promise of possibilities that lay ahead.

And we talked. We talked for an hour, and then two hours, and then I rented the guesthouse. She told me much later that she rented me the place because she knew I needed it.

She's a brilliant woman with world-class beauty. She had been a successful actress in the seventies. But she was also a writer and a sculptor, and had been around the world and on yachts with the jet set in the south of France, and had come full circle to realize that the only thing that matters is the way people treat each other. She was smart and eloquent, two attributes that melt me. This was a remarkable woman.

We were attracted to each other, but we made a decision early on that we shouldn't get involved, that it would not be the smart thing. The idea of having sex with her entered my mind occasionally, but it seemed only to familiarize me with the conflict between my conscience and my desires. I was more excited at the prospect of getting to know her. With sex out of the picture, what she became for me was a "relationship simulator."

I told my friend Peter, "This is the perfect opportunity for me to develop intimacy with a woman without having sex."

And he said, "*Why???*"

Sometimes there's a lot more to be gained by not having sex. Sex can be an escape from intimacy. Sex is easy. Intimacy is hard. Sometimes it's a lot easier to have sex with someone than it is to look him or her in the eyes for five minutes. Actually, most of the time.

When I removed any of the artifice of seduction, I became open to what she was about. I think this was where I really began to start thinking in terms of what I could bring, rather than what I could get. I didn't want anything from this woman. In fact, primarily I wanted her to know that I didn't want anything from her.

She spoke in terms of chivalry and honor and courtship, and I listened. Mostly my time in the house atop the canyon gave me a chance to see a woman be herself. As time passed, I could feel the rhythms of her life and consider the things that were important to her. And I'd ask questions, you know: "What do women want?"

And she said, "Well, first off, the courtship should never end. Too many guys think once they have sex with you, they own you. They give up. They'll take a woman for granted. Then she'll have to spend her time trying to justify herself, and that's a terrible position for a woman to be in—having to defend herself from the man who is supposed to love her."

Hmmm. That sounds familiar.

And finally, after about a year, she said to me, "Michael, I'll *tell* you what women want. Women want a man who likes women."

"Huh?"

"Michael, there are men who like women, and there are men who don't like women. And if a woman is with a man who doesn't like women, she doesn't stand a chance.

"There are men who *like* women and what women say and how they think. They admire the depth of women's feminine nature, and even the little things women do, like the way they put on creams—even if it's taking too long and he's trying to get out the door. And there are men who don't.

"A man like this will seduce a woman for sex, and when the initial sexual intrigue is gone, he'll make her life miserable because he doesn't want to be there in the first place and he feels trapped.

"And the truly insidious thing is that most guys who don't like women don't know they don't like women. You can ask a guy, 'Do you like women?' and he'll say, 'What, are you kidding? I *love* women. Think I'd go to strip clubs twice a week if I didn't like women? Who gets laid more than me? Seriously. Who's a bigger sucker for tits and ass than me?'"

She said, "Do you want to know a great way to tell if a man likes women or not? Watch the way a man mimics a woman's voice while he's telling a story. Because if a woman is listening to a guy tell a story and he starts in with a grating, whining voice, '. . . and then she said, 'Waah, waah, waah . . . ,' she should get the hell out."

Listen to how a man speaks of women. . . .

# TERMINAL ADOLESCENCE

The value and health
of a society is best judged
by the way it treats women,
and children, who are frequently
under women's care.

—STEPHANIE SEGUINO, PH.D.,
associate professor of economics
at the University of Vermont

What the world needs is
a return to sweetness
and decency in the souls
of its young men.
—**AUDREY HEPBURN,**
in Roman Holiday

**M**aybe we weren't paying attention. Maybe we were too busy to notice. It seems to have happened so fast. I don't know when it became okay to call women "bitches" and "whores" and "sluts."

Very early in my life, I learned that anyone who called a girl a bitch or a whore or a slut could be pretty sure her brother would bloody your lip. And rightly so. But that was before Pottersville.

Now it's just commerce. Now you can dehumanize a whole class of people with a broadcast blunderbuss and call it entertainment. But the anonymity of the airwaves makes it no less personal and much more insidious for its spectral evasion of accountability. This degree of degradation against any other class of people would be hate crime. Why has it become acceptable to disparage women? How did this become "amusement"?

Society's benign acceptance of the verbal abuse of women is much the same as its tolerance of the boorish drunk at a dinner party. He's whipping his dick out and pissing in the punch bowl, yelling, "Any woman who doesn't think this is funny is a bitch!" And the men are sidling off toward the den, squeaking, "How about those Mets? Think they have a shot this year?"

The assholes are winning. Any adult who isn't saddened

and appalled by little boys calling eight-year-old girls "bitches" and "hos" is probably making money from it.

**I'm in this business to make money. I never had ratings this high. I never made as much money as I do.**

**—TOM LYKIS,**
syndicated radio "personality"
who has a four-inch dick and refers
to women as bitches, sluts, whores, pigs,
and skanks while giving young men advice
culled from his four failed marriages

Okay. Now that we've perhaps had a little chuckle, for legal reasons I'd just like to say that I don't know how big Tom Lykis's little dick is. But wouldn't it be a great equalizer if men had their dick sizes printed after their names in articles just like women's ages?

Society is littered with sexually arrogant and unprincipled men. Somehow, many of these men have ended up running the advertising industry and controlling our airwaves. The thing that really sucks is they know exactly what they are doing. They've made an educated choice to sell out the beauty of women's souls for two-dimensional ugliness with a fat wallet. Their motivation is simple, whore-based economics.

If you are an advertiser and you want to attract a young male audience, and you know that young males hunger for the approval and acceptance of older males, what's better than filling the airwaves with puerile adult males endorsing sleazy and juvenile behavior? Consequently we end up with 50-year-old frat boys like Howard Stern picking shreds off the carrion of feminine sexual dignity to feed to Infinity Broadcasting shareholders. Yum-yum. Up three dollars.

The real whores are making their money calling women "whores." Ain't that slick?

It's all funny, fellas. "Ha-ha. She's got a fat ass. Look, she's squirming. She's a pig. Hee-hee. Isn't that a hideous ass? Nice jugs, though. Aren't women pathetic? Aren't they sluts?"

Now, thanks to the FCC's dog and pony show, I find myself in the awkward position of having to defend Howard Stern. On the one hand, I hate what Howard Stern has to say about women, and on the other hand, I have to defend his intellectual Skokie. You can't legislate thought. You can't fine somebody out of existence just because you don't like what he has to say. But ultimately what a man decides to contribute to the world is a matter of personal choice. And we all know you can't legislate choice.

There's a much bigger law than the First Amendment that has kept men like Howard Stern and Tom Lykis on the air. It's the law of supply and demand. When ridiculing women to make them more manageable in your frightened-of-girls little-boy brain begins to lose its clubhouse appeal for the millions of men who support it, the marketplace will shed these surrogate abusers.

**Good morning, Anytown! This is the Morning Zoo with Dicky and Danny! Show us your tits!**

*Show us some class, asshole.*

### "I Thought You Had the Kids"

If you were an adolescent male on Pentecost Island in the South Pacific, your exit from childhood would be signaled by a ritual that clearly marks your transition to manhood. A young male climbs a 100-foot wooden platform, and two vines are tied to his ankle. He dives headfirst toward the earth, and when his head gets six inches from the ground, the vine yanks and stops his fall. It's not something easily forgotten, and tethered in his mind to the ceremony that accompanies it, the door to childhood is slammed shut behind him.

We get drunk and get laid. That'll put hair on your chest.

It's hard being a kid these days. There are too many options facing young people today. They are overwhelmed. It's not like it was in the 1860s, when if your father was a carpenter, you became a carpenter. Few sons said, "I have to go find myself, Dad."

Because where would you look? You'd head out into the field, only to return a half-hour later: "I looked. I wasn't there. Gimme the hammer."

Today you don't have to go out looking for your options. Those options will hunt you down. Through your computer, your VCR, your television, and advertising. Every option is a mouse click away. There are no more boundaries of time, distance, custom, and protocol.

Within this information onslaught, too many adult men fail to recognize their responsibility to orient young men to boundaries and restraint. Do you think it's a coincidence that fathers go to strip clubs and their sons are treating little girls like shit? Does it ever occur to frat-boy TV execs and advertising liars that positioning sexual images as the hood ornament of their sales trickery might confuse a young girl who's attempting to find her own self-image as she struggles to adapt to the world of lies adults present her? These people are thieves and con men. They get doctorate degrees in how to manipulate and lie. If the media are the town square of an information society, our common meeting place has lost its leaders—replaced by clever obscurers. Where are the men with a sense of ethics and class? Where are the gentlemen? Why are they quiet? Where the *fuck* is George Bailey?

## The Elephant in the Room

A little over 20 years ago in South Africa, an unanticipated lesson in the importance of adult male guidance in a society began to unfold. Pilanesberg National Park was looking to bring in herds of elephants to stock its new preserve. Coincidentally, Kruger National Park was being overrun by its elephant population, and the difficult decision had been made to cull the herd. But at least the babies could be spared and shipped to Pilanesberg.

Because small elephants are easier to ship, they were transported without adult elephants. The result was that a group of young elephants was placed in a strange environment without the guidance of a mature animal to show them the ropes. They became frightened and anxious.

Enter Randall Moore, a man who bought two female African elephants from a circus in the United States with the intent of freeing them into the wild in Africa. The two females were brought to Pilanesberg, and the desperate youngsters settled down. A strong matriarchal presence seemed to pull the little ones into line and give them the comfort and security they needed.

Ten years passed, and the young male elephants hit puberty. It is a custom for males to be pushed out of the female groups to fend for themselves when they reach adolescence. They usually attach to a bachelor group and hang out with the guys. Except this time there weren't any adult males to guide them and teach them restraint of their burgeoning sexual energies and appetites.

Without more powerful and wiser adult males to keep them in check, and stoked as they were with testosterone, the elephants began to rampage and wreak damage everywhere. Tourists' cars were set upon and pushed around. Next came the savaging of the white rhinos. Pilanesberg is the home to one of six of the world's key populations of white rhinos. In a period of five years, the elephants killed 40 white rhinos. Two tourists also were killed by enraged elephants. It was very clear something had to be done. Someone needed to open a can of whoop-ass.

Several years ago, two adult male elephants were brought into the herd. Since then there have been no outbursts. The adolescent elephants have a few bruises and scrapes from some of the corrective actions taken by their elders. The herd of white rhinos is leading an untroubled existence in its exclusive country club. In the past three years, there hasn't been a single report of an elephant penis denting the back of a Range Rover.

Honestly, I don't think they were actually trying to fuck the motor vehicles, but it's been a few pages since I said anything amusing.

. . .

The positive influence of conscientious men offers balance, identity, and security to our society. The transition to responsible manhood is navigated through a series of difficult choices and the manner in which one responds to them. A man builds his character by consistently making the right moral and ethical choices in situations—regardless of whether those choices happen to be the most profitable or the most comfortable ones. Increasingly, many young men are facing difficult choices with little guidance.

I often hear "bad boy" pro athletes whining, "I never asked to be a role model."

You selfish prick. It's the way life works. Oh, I forgot. You're a rebel. *MTV Cribs* called. You're fabulous.

In *primitive* societies, the adult males usher the young men through the difficult transition to manhood. The young men perceive what is important to the men around them and aspire to that. It's their nature to seek guidance and acceptance. Acceptance and approval quell the terrible feelings of insecurity that accompany adolescence.

Getting laid for the first time or puking your guts out on tequila may be amusing milestones, but they most certainly do not prepare a boy for the difficult transition to manhood. Drinking and predatory sex won't make a boy a man any more than going to a strip club makes someone a "gentleman."

Because the measure of a man won't be found in how many women he can screw or how much beer he can drink or how many doves he can kill.

The measure of a man will be found in how he treats

others. Period. And in his treatment of others the quality of the character he has forged will announce itself.

. . .

Sophocles, as an old man,
was asked if he regretted the loss
of his sexual prowess.

"Not I," he responded.
"Say rather I feel grateful
at having been released from
a stern and relentless taskmaster."

—ISAAC ASIMOV,
from Asimov Laughs Again

## Taming the Beast

The sex drive is not unlike its powerful cousin the atom. It can be harnessed for good, or it can cause terrible destruction.

Most of the men I know strive to do the right thing. Like me, sometimes they don't understand the impact their actions have on others until they've made a mistake and dumbfoundedly witnessed its aftermath. Driven by forces they didn't understand or couldn't control, they created pain in the lives of the people they should have been protecting.

From my experience I believe the challenge that faces every man is to somehow reconcile a naturally unwieldy sex drive with a sense of responsibility to those we love. It's in mastering our impulses and appetites that peace comes to us, and security to our families.

Only trouble is, we have to come to terms with our sex drives amidst a media and advertising culture whose very survival is 100 percent dependent on men continuing to live in their appetites. The tacit message from advertising is that just by virtue of being men, we have sexual entitlement. We deserve what we want, when we want it, no matter what we have to do to get it. I believe that owning a dick entitles me to nothing but a responsibility to govern it.

Hey! I just thought of a name for my penis! "The Constituency."

Damn. I really thought I'd go the distance.

Am I blaming the media for all the temptations they put before men? No. Men have struggled to manage an uncivilized sex drive in a civilized world since they were whacking off to hieroglyphics. But given that men are visually activated, the influence of all the sexual imagery on a man's personal evolution makes the transition from adolescence to responsible manhood very difficult to navigate. In a world where lap dance clubs and rude porn are looked at with a wink and a surrendered "Boys will be boys," some of those boys may remain boys for a long time.

Contrary to what the sign says about "Girls! Girls! Girls!" there are women involved in these men's lives—women perhaps saddened by their man's seeming inability to grow beyond a self-centered teenager.

So no, I don't blame the media. A man playing the victim is an ugly sight to behold. But it's nice to understand the forces that oppose you—all the while backslapping you and flashing a con man's porcelain grin.

With the possible exception of sociopaths, a few TV syndicators, and the soulless hucksters at Abercrombie & Fitch, every man has a spark in his heart that knows what is right. That's why, in spite of all the cultural forces working against our higher natures, there are still so many good men who can power their way through the morass of crap and strive to become their best selves.

Ultimately, the forces outside of us have little significance other than being a distraction. If men look to an illusionary outside world for answers, we will continue to get illusionary answers. There are challenges we need to face, alone in the dark, to learn to channel our strengths. The dragon we have to slay to save the fair maiden is inside of us.

9

# GENTLE
# STRENGTH

## Balance

**I**'m 44 years old now. I don't think that my sex drive has decreased so much as it has become attached to my conscience. There seems to be a balance between my pre-historic desire to inseminate every woman I meet and my ability to move about in a civilized world without leaving wreckage in my wake. My sex drive has become more of a passenger. I've got the wheel now, and I stop to ask for directions.

But it's a stance that goes beyond sexual behaviors. Sexuality is only the first and most obvious layer. It's really an attempt in all areas of my life to find a balance between my selfishness and my consideration of others. The relative manageability of my sex drive is the result of broader work.

Men are born with strengths we spend our lives learning to wrangle. By design we come physically equipped with an ability to do great harm when necessary. If need be, I will kill you to protect my family. However, oftentimes I find myself having to overcome some of my baser instincts—like the impulse to kill you for stealing my parking space. Strength needs to be wielded judiciously.

I think much of being a man is an exercise in reining in the extremes of our nature. We need to be aggressive . . . but not too aggressive. We have to be strong without being overbearing or boorish. Dependable, but not predictable and boring. We need to balance our humor. We have to be kind without being a chump. We have to be vulnerable and open without being insecure or weak.

But I believe there is no balance more important than the ability to direct all of our strengths—sexual or otherwise—with consideration and compassion for others.

It's a gentle strength. It's governed by a man's sense of justice. Superman has gentle strength. What's a sweeter metaphor for idealized manhood than Superman gently cradling a baby in one arm while overpowering evil with the other? And what woman wouldn't want to have a go at the Man of Steel?

Superman is a heroic archetype for a reason. In a world filled with people seeking the easy way out, where it's becoming increasingly difficult to find people you can rely on, a man of strength who embodies higher principle stands out.

We learned about real heroes during 9/11. They're the guys who show up and selflessly do what needs to be done to help others. They are accountable and dependable. Men like these contribute a sense of security to the people around them. They apply their power honorably. They are "go-to" guys.

There are go-to guys, who think about what they can give, and there are "get-away-from" guys, who look for what they can take from situations. Some people are all get and no give. My friend Willy says, "There are two types of people in this world: the people who put their shopping carts back, and the assholes who don't."

In short, there are people who take responsibility and those who act without consideration of others. My friend Bryan describes character as simply "What you will do when no one is watching."

### The Warden

If a man brings gentle strength and responsibility to his relationships, he and the people in his life will flourish. I've heard guys say, "Wow, I was an idiot before I met my wife, but she whipped me into shape. I'm so glad I met her. She got my shit together." They mean it as a compliment, and it's said with gratitude.

I would suggest that it is not a woman's job to "whip you into shape." Unless she's your mother or a schoolteacher or a nun or the warden. It's not her job to give you awarenesses and character you should have acquired before you even met her.

Granted, some awarenesses can be gained only in the relationship. But if you can bring your best self to the situation rather than expect her to whip you into shape, therein lies an extremely important distinction, and quite possibly the survival of your relationship. The difference is whether your initiative to take responsibility cheerfully arises from within as a selfless choice to give or is a whining and reluctant concession to outside forces you resent.

The first shows character; the second shows . . . I don't know . . . but it's weaseling. It's the difference between being a man and a boy. And a boy needs a mom.

If you go into a relationship thinking she's going to help make you into something, there is a very strong possibility you may not like what she makes you into. Or the methods she uses. And then she becomes, in your limited estimation, a "bitch."

Nothing frustrates guys like when a woman says disapprovingly, "If you don't know what's bothering me, I'm not going to tell you." It drives us nuts.

Perhaps this is what she isn't telling you:

"It's not my responsibility to constantly monitor the relationship and ride herd on you. In addition to not meeting your responsibilities, you blame me for seeing it. The reason I'm not telling you is because I'm tired of you rolling your eyes, getting sarcastic, or looking to blame me every time I try to tell you something I shouldn't have to tell you in the first place. This is not the love I was looking for."

You've turned her into the Warden, and then you get upset every time you hear a set of keys rattling down the hall. She knows that no matter how much she tries to explain that to you, if you're a blamer, you will never look at the possibility that you created the problem. How do you tell someone who's not listening that the problem is they're not listening? Ignorance is its own denial.

It's not her job to tell you to take responsibility. Any man who calls a woman a bitch is likely witnessing her frustration at his having created by omission an emotional environment where she has to become the other half of the half a man he is, *and then get blamed for it.*

You'd be a little pissed, too.

I'm not ignoring the fact that there are actually some pretty mean women out there. Not all women are made of sugar and spice and everything nice. There are individual women who are hard and mercenary and out to get whatever they can. There are individual women who treat people like shit. But do I think it's women's nature to be hardened and cynical? Do I look at a little girl and believe that it is her nature to grow up angry and cynical? No. It's acquired.

We're not born with baggage. We pick up defense techniques on a need-to-know basis. As we encounter experiences that threaten our safety and peace of mind, we develop layers of survival skills. If a girl grows up in a physically or emotionally abusive home, if her father deserted the family, if "Daddy is scary when he drinks," if a relative or neighbor breaks sacred trust, or if every message a girl gets is that her value is to be found only in her sexuality as it relates to men's needs, where is her opportunity to live outside of the only experience she knows? Some women learn early that if they don't look out for themselves, no one else will. If their accrued experience shows them that men are not to be trusted, why wouldn't they become skeptical and anticipate further disappointment? Is it profiling? No. Just good police work.

Lack of forgiveness and the anticipation of further disappointment block women from seeing their possibilities. Men's rush to categorically and dismissively judge these women continues the oppression unreliable men have set into motion. I have tremendous trouble blaming women for their pain.

If women and children hit potholes going down the only roads the men in their lives have built, is it any surprise when a few wheels get knocked out of alignment? The question is, will men continue to complain about the bumpy ride?

Or will we try to build better roads?

■ ■ ■

**First, do no harm.**
**—HIPPOCRATIC OATH**

It takes more courage to reveal
insecurities than to hide them,
more strength to relate to people
than to dominate them,
more "manhood" to abide by
thought-out principles rather than
blind reflex. Toughness is in
the soul and spirit, not in muscles
and an immature mind.

**—ALEX KARRAS,**
actor and five-time All Pro linebacker
for the Detroit Lions

## Creating Safety

When Mike Tyson was arrested in Indiana for raping a beauty contestant, I remember thinking, Of all the people in his entourage—this guy had the biggest entourage I'd ever seen—there wasn't one guy who could have said, "Gee, Mike, maybe you shouldn't treat women that way." They were either brought up with the same ethos as he, or they were financially dependent on Mike and afraid to say what was right—so instead, they shrugged or chuckled over and over, one way or another, through the years. Mike's attitudes and behaviors toward women grew gradually, tacitly endorsed by yes-men.

Grown men in Mike Tyson's life failed that young woman. The wink and nod, the resigned shrug, the acceptance of lower standards of ethics are ruining our lives and the lives of those around us. There is nothing cute, there is nothing funny, about treating women poorly.

What if all men considered it of primary importance to create an environment where the gentler among us could be safe from those who would hurt them? What if children could live a fully innocent childhood without being cynically targeted for their buying power or hit in the indiscriminate cross fire of sexually driven drive-by marketing? What if better treatment of women and children were more important to men than the Super Bowl, the stock market, a lap dance, owning the right car, getting paid, or getting laid? How would our world change if women and children felt safe?

It's no longer a question of "What is 'society' going to do about it?" We're witnessing what "society" has been able to do about it. We can't turn on the television or leave our houses without witnessing what society has been able to do about it. What if each man chose to expect better from himself and his fellows and to set that example for young men?

A man's power should be wielded compassionately. Whether it is the power of his fists or the power of the airwaves, each man should be accountable for the effect he has on the world, regardless of how many degrees of separation may cloak his participation.

Until our side of the street is clean, how can we judge women so harshly when they respond to injustices that unprincipled men have set into motion? Many of the same men who are so quick to bully women by labeling them "bitches" behave like drunken trust fund–fueled schoolboys with overblown senses of entitlement and disregard for the feelings of others. Then they'll blame women's lib for confusing men's roles and emasculating them.

The truth is that a man's choice to pursue irresponsible behavior also surrenders his claim to true power and to any right he has to judge the actions of those who do what they must to live amidst the wreckage created by irresponsible men.

"Gentle strength" sounds like a contradiction. But the effective convergence of power and gentility is the target the heat-seeking missile seeks. It's where the animal meets one's humanity. It's the mastery of dualism. It's evolution.

Overriding base desires and selfish impulse with high principle is not always the easiest road to take. But that's the challenge that faces each man. And that challenge well-met is an art. It's the art of the gentleman.

# INTIMACY

I read everywhere that it's
perfectly normal to fantasize that
your sex partner is someone else.
You spend your entire adolescence
having sex alone, wishing you
had a sex partner. Then, when you
finally get someone . . . you pretend
they're somebody else. This can only
mean that when you get too old to
have sex, all you can do is reminisce
about all the people you really never
had sex with in the first place.

### "Did Ya Give Any?"

Sometimes it seems like I've spent the first half of my life making mistakes and the second half trying to correct them. I tried to do the best I could with the information I had, but a lot of what I had learned was inadequate or wrong. I think many of my errors could have been avoided had I just been told one simple thing about women and relationships. One simple thing: You don't *get* laid; you *give* laid.

Once I start to think about what I can bring instead of what I can get, many of my problems disappear. I am no longer competing for anything. I no longer "deserve" anything. If a sense of humor is "right-sized thinking," then living in the mind-set of what I can bring to a situation is "right-sized feeling." Because anything else is fear. It's fear of losing what I have or of not getting what I want.

One of the most important things I can bring to a relationship is a willingness to put aside everything I think I know to make room for a brand-new experience. Oftentimes our preconceptions—many of which were formed in adolescence—of what we think women should be will block us from experiencing what women really are.

### Creativity

When I was a teenager, I considered masturbation "rehearsal." I was rehearsing for when the real thing came along. But there comes a time when you have to ask yourself, "When the curtain goes up opening night, do I want to be Laurence Olivier? Or will I be Steven Seagal?"

I've been told I'm somewhere near Rick Moranis in *Ghost-*

*busters*, but the point is . . . all of my sex growing up was theoretical. I spent much time thinking about sex. How I was going to get it and what I was going to do with it when I got it. During the early years of my awareness, my sex life was entirely in my mind. Which was probably a good place for it, given my ignorance.

Throughout my teenage years, my imagination and my sex drive spent a lot of time together. After a while, they became inseparable, forming a bond that would last a lifetime. Like Bogie and Bacall. Tracy and Hepburn. Jackson and Presley. Scratch that last one.

Now, the imagination is a great thing. Man's ability to visualize has enabled him to create beautiful things. Art. Sculpture. Literature. Music. The humanities. Forward-thinking idealists have written volumes about imagined utopias. We envision great buildings and structures. We design marvels of engineering. We build huge bridges so we can have sex on the other side of the river.

But the very same unbridled imagination that helps us visualize greatness can also blind us from seeing what is actually there. Our imagination can create a hell of an agenda that will block us from intimacy. It can rob the other person of the ability to participate.

Fantasy served me well when I was having sex with magazines. But if I want sexual intimacy, I need to relinquish some degree of fantasy in order for my spirit to be available. If women are expected to let go of the simplistic childhood fantasy that Prince Charming is going to whisk them away to live happily ever after, men need to drop the fantasy that Cinderella and Snow White are both going to go down on us at the same time.

The beginning of love is to let
those we love be perfectly themselves,
and not to twist them to fit
our own image. Otherwise, we love
only the reflection of ourselves
we find in them.

**—THOMAS MERTON**

## Just Her

While men's magazines sell men the fantasy that they will get to have sex with the perfect airbrushed woman, women's magazines are marketed to a woman's fear that she will never be able to compete with that perfect airbrushed woman.

When I see interviews with the world's most beautiful women, they all thought they were ugly when they were teens, and *still* have features they hate. I can only begin to imagine the unrealistic pressures young women feel to measure up. They will never be able to compete with computerized perfection, but they will die of bulimia trying. Whatever it takes.

The good news is if they follow the tips in the articles, they'll be shown how to get a man to like them in spite of their tremendous inadequacies. Never mind which man. Just get one. Now! What are you doing reading this? Go get a man!

I would love to go to a newsstand one day and all the men's magazines would say, "Sorry, no pictures of naked women this month. You jerk off too much." And the women's magazines say, "Ah . . . you look okay. You look fine. Relax, it's cool."

Everywhere women look, they get messages that they are not enough. Within my relationship do I want to be yet another source of those messages, or do I want the emotional environs of our relationship to be the one place where she can go to feel safe?

Here's where my fantasizing mechanism intersects with a woman's intuition and unwittingly tweaks at her sense of security and erodes a sexual relationship. To the exact extent that my imagination lives in the desire of what I don't have, it implies that the woman I am with is not enough. She is going to feel both my dissatisfaction and the lack of my presence. No amount of trying to convince her that everyone else is doing something is going to change the way she feels—lonely during sex. Love is supposed to be where we can go to feel good.

I figure the best thing I can do is lose my expectations and two-dimensional fantasies and just let her be herself. Where she stands now. In the clothing she wears now. At the weight she's at now. There is nothing more beautiful than a woman who flourishes being just the woman she is.

Not Hugh Hefner's idea of a woman. Not Howard Stern's idea of a woman. Not Larry Flynt's idea of a woman. Not the girl in the music video portrayed as the slave to men's desires. Not the bitch or the ho in rap songs. Not the beer advertisers' girl who fucks me in 15 seconds because I chose Michelob over Miller. Not the fantasy blueprint I came up with when I was 14. Not the woman who spins out and loses herself trying to fit the image of what she thinks men think a woman should be. And not the warden.

Just her.

In the last analysis, everything I think I know about men

and women doesn't matter. It's all theory and old ideas. In practical application, the idea of "men and women" is an illusion and an intrusion. It's not "men and women." It's just "me and her."

Picture a room. Inside is all my baggage from ex-girlfriends, my seventh-grade gym teacher Mr. Groh, Jimmy Kelly and the rest of my misguided education, that bully Tom Lykis, hookers, porn stars, strippers, blaring music calling women whores. My soul mate walks in. I can barely see her through the crowd. I can't hear a word she's saying.

Now picture a different room. Empty. It's quiet. She walks in. All I see is her. She comes closer. I can feel her breathe. I intuitively know that this room is exactly where I am supposed to be. My hand reaches to lock the door.

It's "me and her." Two people. Trying to make a little love and find some comfort in an all too often harsh world.

## Passion

There is a love that transcends trend and happenstance. It is a timeless love that lives beyond language and the fleeting whims of fad. It is the powerful feeling of joy that fills us when we witness the birth of a baby, the beauty of a sunrise, or a triumph of human spirit. It touches the heart and excites the soul. It has been the muse for poets, artists, musicians, and writers for thousands of years. It is a nonsexual love that at once fills us to bursting and makes us hunger to share it with another.

When sex is used to express this love, it is atomic. It's one of the most beautiful, powerful, and fulfilling experiences on earth. You bring each other to the place in your hearts where your smiles come from, where your joy lives, and you touch it and your souls touch. It is both infinite and intimate. It is a deep, raw, passionate intimacy, and you look each other in the eyes when you come and start crying at the beauty of it. For a moment there is no fear, there is no time, and there is nothing but the absolute sense that you have communed in a place you are extremely fortunate to have gotten to.

And the day after you go there, she tries to pick a fight.

## Testing

True intimacy reminds us of our vulnerability. Whether it's conscious or unconscious, a woman will ask herself, "If he can't protect himself from me, how's he going to protect me from the rest of the world?"

In an ideal world, she wouldn't have to test you. And bottled drinking water wouldn't cost more than gasoline. In an ideal world, we would all be able to experience the beauty and purity and abandonment of intimate love without having to worry about protecting ourselves. But that ain't the world we live in, I say, sipping a two-dollar bottle of Evian.

Relationships are a lot like drugs. You develop a dependency. Also, if you're not really careful, you can end up losing your house.

We've all been hurt, and we've all got battle scars. Love is trial and error. Mostly error. We've all got baggage and fears. And fear of baggage. And issues. Some people subscribe, and receive a new issue in the mail every month.

The question that faces each of us when we have an opportunity to fall in love again is "Am I willing to risk taking another bullet?"

Given our history of failed relationships and the pain that ensues, is it any wonder that we have to proceed with caution? But how much caution is too much caution? My friend Dave took a woman to couples therapy on their first date. He told her, "Look. We're going to end up here anyway; let's just get it over with."

By definition, for every relationship that didn't work out, a woman has had to protect herself in one way or another from every man who's ever gotten close—or she's ended up kicking herself for not protecting herself.

So when she falls newly in love, her joy immediately slingshots into a directly proportional apprehension: "When's he going to screw this up? If it feels *this* good, it's going to feel *that* bad. I'd better not let my guard down."

The only way she can begin to let her guard down is to find out what you're made of. She has to ask herself, "Does this man have the kind of character that wants what is best for me, or is he an opportunist? Is his seduction dishonest?" The truly insidious aspect of dishonest seduction is that it enters the woman's life mimicking love. It's a Trojan horse, so to speak.

It's no secret men have a rap for talking a good game. "Great sales team, but when it breaks down, just try getting the service department on the line."

Only the passage of time will tell if a man's actions will back up his words. But there is a way to speed up the screening process. She can push you away.

A man may react indignantly to this. "Hey! Why should I have to pay for all the crap the guys before me did?"

Are you at all responsible for any of those bad relationships she chose? Absolutely not. You didn't break it; you can't fix it.

But now it's a whole new ball game, and you are up at bat. A curveball is headed straight for your face. At first glance it appears to be something scary you had better get away from quickly. Will you stand in the bucket and wait for the curve to break, or are you going to duck like a chump and blame the ump when it skims the inside corner for a called strike three?

It has to be waited out with patient dignity. For her.

There comes a point where one realizes that sometimes the most loving thing a man can do for a woman is *not* seduce her. He'll have sex with fewer women, but the trade-off is that the quality improves.

For him, too.

And on a societal level, just think about how a sexually ethical approach to women helps out mankind. If each of us leaves a little less wreckage in his path, everyone will have less baggage and less cynicism and more openness and we'll all live happily ever after. All because Stuey didn't nail that drunk girl at the frat party when he had the chance.

It's unrealistic to think that you can have sex with every woman. But it's realistic, and more fulfilling, to be admired by all women for the way you treat one of them. Women love having something every other woman desires but can't have. Think "shoes."

## Possibilities

What amazes me is the resilience we all have. No matter how much or how many times we've been hurt, so many of us continue to bounce back. We still risk taking another bullet because we know love exists. We have felt it, however briefly, and we have felt it leave. We know it exists because we've touched it.

One of the things that make new romance and courtship so appealing is that they give us a chance to live in possibilities. Fear subsides within a willingness to believe there is hope ahead. New love offers us an opportunity to dream; a chance to look past what is, to what could be. God bless the people who continue to believe in love in spite of their hurt.

In the immediate wake of September 11, *Vanity Fair* editor Graydon Carter declared it "the death of irony" and was roundly ridiculed—probably because death-defying firemen don't respond to crisis with an impulse to have tea with Oscar Wilde.

I would hope rather it marked the death of cynicism. Cynics blew up the World Trade Center. We could use some hope and trust and humor that celebrates and enriches our often frail lives, not degrades them. We have had enough hurt.

The question "What do women want?" is timeless, and so, I believe, is the answer. Women want what they've always wanted—before their physical and sexual idiosyncrasies were debased and exploited by advertisers, magazine publishers, television executives, pornographers, and emotionally retarded DJs.

They want to feel safe. They'd like to see kindness, consideration, integrity, and they'd like to be able to find trust where they expect it to be. The truth of the universe hasn't changed just because the lies have gone into syndication.

This observation is not a big stretch. The desire to feel safe is certainly not gender specific; it's a fundamental human need. We are all a lot more vulnerable than we'd like to admit—or, as is sadly ironic for many men, more vulnerable than we feel safe admitting. Nearly every man I know has fears accompanied by a strong sense of conditioning that he is not permitted to have fears.

Fear of appearing ignorant or weak in front of women has blocked men from intimacy, from a woman's gentle love, and from fully participating in our lives since adolescence. It blocks us from learning from women and creates untold frustration for people in our lives.

The manner in which we deal with our "socially unacceptable fears" controls our relationships and blocks our partners from attaining the intimacy they crave.

Here's a rough sketch of how my fear of intimacy has manifested itself, to one degree or another, my entire life. My pride wields bluster and bravado it thinks will keep my vulnerabilities from being discovered, for fear of being rejected by an abstraction of a judgmental woman that's been created in my mind and the collective minds of men around me. But ironically, my own self-involvement in this process is distracting *me* from realizing that she had long ago seen what I am struggling to hide and "could we move on together through this limited pattern to a less frustrating and more fulfilling level of exchange, please?"

Sometimes I think my brain has a mind of its own.

Ten years ago, when I admitted to myself that I had a lot more to learn and needed to make the effort to do it, my life began to open up. I was willing to throw out the old ideas that didn't work to make room for something richer and more fulfilling for myself and for a lover who would someday enter my life. I've found that merely the attitude of being open to receive and grow was enough to begin to change my life. I have a feeling that's the "listening" women keep asking for.

I've heard it said that of marriages that fail, something like 85 percent fail over money issues. I would guess that there wasn't one of those where much earlier on, each partner hadn't said, "I don't feel heard."

True intimacy has a willingness to listen. To listen to each other's words, their ideas, to their heartbeats, to their rhythms. Intimacy means dropping the mask and being open, especially during sex. Isn't it ironic that we often hide most when we are physically closest? True intimacy means being present and available.

I've heard guys say, "It's not the size of the ship; it's the motion of the ocean." Well, none of that stuff matters if the captain's not on board.

In fact, if two lovers are completely present and open, it is possible to remain virtually motionless and be the best lover each has ever had. Because deeply intimate sex is the expression and exchange of spirits. If great sex is like exploring Paris, tantric sex is the Palace of Versailles.

Not that motion isn't important. I'm just distinguishing layers here—no pun intended. Motion is very important. I was in the grocery store last week, and the guy in front of me in the express checkout line was buying a dozen condoms and Gatorade.

It's important to set goals in life.

Casual sex is fine if that's what you want. But it ceased being fulfilling for me way before it ceased. Even the term *casual* sounds so empty and impersonal. "Casual" is like "By the way . . ." or "Incidentally." "Did I mention my penis is in you? I was in the neighborhood; thought I'd drop in. This isn't a bad time, is it? I could come back."

# ZUZU'S
# PETALS

## New Life

**O**ne of my greatest fears in life, ranking third behind death and mimes, has always been that I will get to the end of my life and discover I had completely missed the point.

At 44 years old, I feel like I'm starting to understand what life is about. I feel like I've come to a place of relative balance and minor wisdom. But I also have enough experience to understand that two years from now, I'll probably look back on now and realize I knew nothing.

When I was 18, I was cocky. I thought I had the world by the balls. I believed I had it together. I was something. Then I hit 21—I *knew* I had it together at 21—but I looked back at 18 and wondered, "What the hell was I thinking?"

At 25 I thought I finally had the right take on life. I looked back at 21 and thought, "Jeez. I was out of my mind when I was 21."

Now I look back at 25 the same way. And 30. And 35.

I wonder if somewhere there is a 90-year-old man saying, "You know, when I was 87 . . . I was *clueless*. But *thank God* now I am finally living up to my potential. I'll tell you something . . . if I only knew at 87 what I know now at 90, I would do it all differently."

. . .

It's now been 10 years since that sunny morning I drove my motorcycle up into Laurel Canyon and rented that cottage. I lived there for a year and a half, and everything has changed since then. Susan, the woman I rented the house from, has become a lifelong friend. Linda has become a distant memory. I am fortunate to have someone in my life now who loves me unconditionally. She is open, communicates her needs very clearly, and has no baggage. She's 11 months old.

She's just beginning to walk. She says a few words, like "daddy," "mommy," "kitty." I am pretty sure yesterday morning she said, "Trust fund."

I met her mom four years ago, and I was willing to take a bullet. I would have taken tracer fire and a mortar. Our daughter was conceived in Scotland while we were at the Edinburgh Festival for my show. We were trying to have a baby. Relationships are give-and-take. Shari really wanted a baby; I really wanted a motorcycle. It sounded like this could work out real nice for both of us. Now we've had the baby and—yes, that's right—I can't have a motorcycle because I have to be responsible. But I have a baby girl.

When I was younger, I plowed my will through people's lives to try to get what I wanted. I had plans. Whenever the topic of having kids would come up in conversation, I'd say, "I like to consider myself the architect of my destiny, and children would spill ink on the blueprints." Because for eight years I thought I was Dorothy Parker.

With the benefit of hindsight, a little wisdom, a loving woman, and a beautiful baby girl in my life, I realize that my blueprints more often blocked rewards in my life than reached them. And I am very clearly not the architect. Not even close.

Most of my life when I heard the word *commitment* used in the context of marriage vows, I always thought it to mean simply a promise to not have sex with another woman. I've learned that it's a commitment to build something together and take equal responsibility to continue nurturing that shared vision. It's a commitment to uphold my side of things no matter what. It's taking responsibility to provide an environment of trust and consistency so the people in my life can flourish. It means no bonehead moves. It means that when I tell her "Everything's going to be all right," she knows she can believe me. And I can believe me. "Pencils down; test over."

**fore·play** (fōr-plā, fòr-) 1929 n.
1. sexual stimulation prior to intercourse.
2. action or behavior that precedes an event.

Maybe foreplay isn't just what a man does to get a woman sexually excited in the moments before intercourse. Maybe it's closer to that second definition, and foreplay is all of a man's actions and behavior when he's *not* having sex with a woman.

Maybe foreplay is in the way he nurtures her and in the things he does to create trust so she'll feel safe. Maybe it's not just "foreplay" but also "during-play" and "after-play" and "the-things-you-do-when-you're-away-and-no-one's-watching-play." Maybe it's in the way he listens to her concerns and honors her dreams. Perhaps it's in the actions he takes to hone his character before he even meets her.

Foreplay could be in the actions and behavior he doesn't do. It could be when he makes an effort to not be sarcastic. Maybe it's the night he forgoes the strip club to stay home and draw her a hot bath or read to his children. Maybe it's in his willingness to believe that just because something is what he has always done, or is what many others are doing, doesn't make it right.

Years ago I set out to answer the questions "What makes a man?" and "What do women want?" and I've found that the answers to the first question are pretty much the same as the answers to the second one. Somewhere along the way, it occurred to me that I didn't have to figure out women in order to be happy. I had to figure myself out, and the rest would follow. It was never about finding the right woman. It was about becoming the right man.

## ACKNOWLEDGMENTS

**N**o man is an island. However, John Holmes was a peninsula. Herewith a partial list of people who have made my life and this book better. If I've omitted anyone, I'm sorry.

Shari, whom I mentioned earlier, deserves a little elaboration here. She put up with the "kid with a dream" crap for longer than tolerance should be tested. I love her and the children she's brought into our life. (One more after the book was written!)

I was lucky to grow up with my parents, brother, and sisters. My mom, Maude, is one of the smartest women I've ever met. She could rip your throat out in Scrabble. Raymond Stephen Dugan is as principled a man as there ever was.

Thanks to Rory Rosegarten, for spending 20 years building the kind of reputation that gets manuscripts looked at by the right people: my agent at William Morris, Mel Berger; and my editor at Rodale, Leah Flickinger, who has just the right touch.

My life has been blessed with Susan Benton, an angel and muse. I am lucky to have worked with my friend Anne

Beatts, who has the best comedy-writing instincts I've ever witnessed. Kevin Rooney is a great writer and a great friend. If I were that smart, I'd be dead. John Magnuson has always shown me unconditional love and he has great stories about Lenny Bruce. He also wrote the Rice-a-Roni jingle. Paul Provenza has supported me from the moment I hit the stage. Bob Fisher did more for my development as a comedian than any one person. Thanks to Marsha and Robin Williams for always being there and showing me what's important.

My two years writing and performing in England would not have been the joy they were without Jon Keyes, Steven Alan Green, and Peter Thompson, a great author who, among many other things, helped me prepare the script for the Edinburgh Festival.

Jimmy Demers' encouragement during the writing of this book helped contribute to its voice. Thanks to Ellie and Barry Goldstein, Scott LaRose, Jeff Dordick, Andy Horowitz, Alix and Budd Friedman, Eleanor Jones, Ellen and Dulce Farmer, Kathryn Nyce, Turk O'Connor, Harvey Jason, Eric Lee Wright, and The BHMS. I hope some of the ideas in this book honor what all these people have given me.